THE GIRL ON THE TRAIN

Paula Hawkins's

THE GIRL ON THE TRAIN

A stage play by Rachel Wagstaff and Duncan Abel

OBERON BOOKS
LONDON

WWW.OBERONBOOKS.COM

First published in 2018 by Oberon Books Ltd
521 Caledonian Road, London N7 9RH
Tel: +44 (0) 20 7607 3637 / Fax: +44 (0) 20 7607 3629
e-mail: info@oberonbooks.com
www.oberonbooks.com

A catalogue record for this book is available from the British
Library.

PB ISBN: 9781786825124
E ISBN: 9781786825131

Cover image: Bob King Creative

Printed and bound by 4EDGE Limited, Hockley, Essex, UK.
eBook conversion by CPI Group (UK) Ltd, Croydon, CR0 4YY.

The authors would like to thank:
Simon Friend, Joe Murphy, Paula Hawkins, Georgina Ruffhead,
Rose Cobbe, Dan Usztan, the cast and crew
and West Yorkshire Playhouse

Based on the best-selling novel by
Paula Hawkins and the DreamWorks film

Adapted by Rachel Wagstaff & Duncan Abel

A West Yorkshire Playhouse production
in association with Simon Friend

First performance at West Yorkshire Playhouse on 12 May 2018

Cast
Jill Halfpenny – Rachel Watson
Adam Best – Tom Watson
Florence Hall – Megan Hipwell
Jonas Khan – Kamal Abdic
Theo Ogundipe – Scott Hipwell
Sarah Ovens – Anna Watson
Colin Tierney – D.I. Gaskill

Creative Team
Director – Joe Murphy
Designer – Lily Arnold
Lighting Designer – Lizzie Powell
Sound Designer and Composer – Isobel Waller-Bridge
Assistant Director – Laurence Young
Fight Directors – Rachel Bown-Williams
and Ruth Cooper-Brown of Rc-Annie Ltd.
Casting Director – Gabrielle Dawes

Characters

RACHEL WATSON

D.I. GASKILL

ANNA WATSON

MEGAN HIPWELL

TOM WATSON

SCOTT HIPWELL

KAMAL ABDIC

Other characters should be played
by members of the cast

Authors' note

/   indicates where a line overlaps

…   indicates a trailing off, or a pause for thought

–   indicates an interruption

Sections in **bold** indicate a memory or the recounting
of action which has previously taken place.

Act One

PRE-SET

The mouth of a tunnel, from which there is no light.

Overhead, railway lines. Danger signs. In the foreground, the grassy, thistly, unkempt no man's land that lies between the railway line and the back gardens. Discarded clothes, beer cans, a child's doll. A small pile of stones.

The sound of trains flying past: loud, breathtaking, horns. Blue sparks, from overhead wires.

In the tunnel: RACHEL, she is disoriented. Blurred, muffled voices. The sound of glass smashing. RACHEL collapses.

SCENE ONE

RACHEL's apartment. Empty bottles of wine, unwashed glasses, dinner plates with half-eaten food, a few G&T cans strewn around. A Waitrose carrier bag.

RACHEL is lying, crumpled.

Suddenly, there is someone at the door.

RACHEL gets to her feet. Pulls herself together. She goes to the door.

RACHEL: Yes?

GASKILL: *(Showing her his badge.)* Detective Gaskill. May I…?

> *She allows him in.*

RACHEL: I'm sorry, I'm a bit of a – *it's* a bit of a mess.

> *GASKILL comes in. RACHEL begins a quick tidy up. She starts to pick up the drinks cans.*

GASKILL: Been having a party?

RACHEL: No. I mean, yes. But they've gone. My friends, they've all – I was just clearing up.

GASKILL: You're Rachel Watson?

RACHEL: What have I done?

GASKILL: It's a missing person. She lives on your old road. Blenheim Road.

RACHEL: Why would you know where I used to live?

GASKILL: Your husband – sorry, *ex*-husband's *new* wife gave me your address.

RACHEL: Anna?

GASKILL: You know her?

RACHEL: No.

GASKILL: Oh. She said you call the house quite a lot.

RACHEL: I know of her. I just don't know her.

> *Beat.*

RACHEL: Who's the missing person?

GASKILL: Her name's Megan Hipwell. Do you know her?

RACHEL: I don't think so, no.

GASKILL: She used to run the art gallery, on Roseberry Avenue.

> *GASKILL produces a photograph.*

RACHEL: I'm sorry. I've never –

> *RACHEL takes the photograph. As she looks at it:*

> **MEGAN appears.**

> **RACHEL looks at her. A shocked look of recognition on RACHEL's face.**

> **MEGAN disappears.**

RACHEL: I'm sorry, I don't know a Megan *(puts down the photograph)*.

GASKILL: Are you sure? She lives two doors down from your ex-husband.

RACHEL: She must have moved there after I left. I didn't know her – *don't* know her. I'm not saying she's…

GASKILL: I'm speaking to people who were in the vicinity when she disappeared. Where were you Saturday night?

RACHEL: Here.

GASKILL: The big party…

They both smile.

GASKILL: So, you weren't at Blenheim Road?

RACHEL: No.

GASKILL: *(Writes in his notepad.)* The only thing is, the new Mrs Watson, she said you *were* there Saturday night.

RACHEL: But, but I wasn't. She must be…

GASKILL: …?

RACHEL: Lying. She must be lying.

GASKILL: Why would she –

RACHEL: She –

GASKILL: She was certain you'd come to her house Saturday night.

RACHEL: *(Still confused.)* That doesn't make any sense. Saturday, I –

What did Anna say about me?

ANNA appears, holding her baby. The conversation ANNA had with GASKILL is replayed.

ANNA: **She's completely obsessed with us. She phones and hangs up. She turns up unannounced. She even took our baby once. Did you know that?**

ANNA caresses baby EVIE. Holds her close.

GASKILL: **What did this Rachel want Saturday night?**

ANNA: **To see Tom. Again. I told her he was at the gym.**
She'd been drinking. Tears, make-up all over her face. Evie was frightened. Rachel was threatening me.

3

I've tried so hard to be understanding, but there has to be a limit...

GASKILL: **Did she try to hurt you?**

ANNA: **I don't know what she's capable of. I don't even think she does.**

GASKILL: **Did she try to hurt you?**

ANNA: **No. But...she called, later. Left some rambling message for Tom.**

ANNA disappears.

GASKILL turns back to RACHEL.

GASKILL: So, which one of you is lying?

RACHEL: That's not true. I was here. I had a couple of drinks, and then I –

The penny drops.

Oh...

GASKILL: Rachel?

RACHEL: No. She's right.

I'd had a few drinks. I wasn't planning to... I just wanted to see him. My husband.

GASKILL: Ex-husband.

RACHEL: But I didn't threaten her. I went home. Bought some more drink and had a... *(She looks at all the mess.)*

GASKILL: Party?

RACHEL: ... Yes.

GASKILL: For one.

RACHEL: But I didn't call them later. Didn't leave a message.

Beat.

RACHEL: Did I?

We hear the message played. RACHEL drunk and teary.

RACHEL: *(On the voicemail.)* **Tom. I'm really sorry about coming round tonight. I just wanted to see you. My**

landlord, he… I didn't mean to cause a scene. I don't know why Anna has to be such a – sorry. I'm sorry. *(Beeps.)*

Silence.

RACHEL: I didn't mean to lie. I promise.

I get these…sort of, black holes in my memory. I wake up the next day and people have to tell me what happened… what I did.

GASKILL: A medical condition? Or…?

They both look at all the booze.

RACHEL: So, I drink. Sometimes people need something just to…

Okay, I was there. But I didn't see Jess.

GASKILL: Jess?

RACHEL: Megan. Sorry. I didn't see Megan.

GASKILL: But you'd been drinking…

RACHEL: …

GASKILL: So, what kind of drinker are you? A Waitrose drinker?

RACHEL: What d'you mean?

GASKILL: My old dad, he'd sway down the street with a bottle of wine in a brown paper bag and people crossed over to avoid him. Someone walks down the road with their wine in a Waitrose bag, people think they're part of a civilised society. But it all ends up the same. The need.

RACHEL: Yes, well, I'm not –

GASKILL: And that's when things are going well. Then you get the redundancy. No job, but the need of a drink is still there. Still get it from Waitrose until the money's gone. Then you're in Bargain Booze, with the rest of us, working out the cost per unit of alcohol, and now people are crossing the road to avoid *you.*

RACHEL: So what type of drinker are you?

GASKILL: Recovered.

What happened here?

GASKILL goes to touch a cut on RACHEL's head. Suddenly, there's a change of light.

GASKILL: Rachel?

RACHEL: I remember something.

RACHEL moves to the tunnel.

RACHEL: I was in the underpass, near Blenheim Road.

I felt a –

Lights, sound, music shift. RACHEL feels a blow to her head. The sound of a glass bottle smashing. RACHEL goes down.

RACHEL gets to her feet. Her hands go to her head. Blood on her hands. RACHEL staggers out of the tunnel.

Back to present day:

GASKILL: Someone attacked you?

RACHEL: I had blood on my head. My hands.

GASKILL: Did you attack anyone?

RACHEL: Why would I do that?

GASKILL: Was the blood on your hands from your head, or…?

RACHEL: I don't know. It must have been. I don't remember anything else.

GASKILL: The black holes in your memory.

RACHEL: I'm sorry. Am I a suspect?

GASKILL: For all I know, she might have run away with the circus. I just need to know if you saw anything that might help us.

RACHEL has nothing left to say.

GASKILL: Come on. Let me help you clear some of this up.

GASKILL and RACHEL begin loading the Waitrose bag with the rubbish. GASKILL picks up a letter. RACHEL goes to stop him, but it's too late.

GASKILL: Eviction notice. Two weeks…

RACHEL: I'm sorting it out. Just a misunderstanding.

GASKILL: I don't think I've found you at a very good time, have I?

RACHEL: I'm fine.

Beat.

GASKILL: If you remember anything more about Saturday night.

GASKILL goes to hand her his card, but remembers something.

GASKILL: Why did you take Anna Watson's baby that time?

RACHEL: It wasn't like that…

Beat.

GASKILL: *(Hands her the card. Takes the bag.)* Here, I'll take this out for you.

GASKILL leaves. RACHEL spots the photograph of MEGAN. Picks it up. Goes to call after GASKILL. Doesn't.

SCENE TWO

TOM appears with his gym bag. Post workout. RACHEL has cornered him outside the gym.

RACHEL: What's Anna been telling the police?

TOM: What are you doing here?

RACHEL: The detective, he said –

Is that a fake tan?

TOM: No.

RACHEL: It is! Why are you fake tanning!? Is it for Anna?

TOM: I've been promoted at work. A new team…

RACHEL: And they want your skin to be more orange?

TOM: I'm just trying to fit in. Each floor you go up in the office, the people become more beautiful. It's like a fucking game show. Why have you come here?

RACHEL: Because if I go to your house, your wife –

TOM: No. I mean, what do you want?

RACHEL: That detective, he thinks I threatened Anna.

TOM: You did threaten Anna.

RACHEL: I just came round to see you. She was the one who –
Oh, God. She was fake-tanned as well. Do you do it together?

TOM: Look, he wanted to know if we'd seen anyone the night Megan Hipwell disappeared. Not to have mentioned you would have looked like there was something to hide. I've got to get going.

RACHEL: Do you know the woman? Megan?

TOM: Yeah. She used to look after Evie sometimes.

RACHEL: Can't Anna cope with her own baby?

TOM: That's not fair. *(Turns to go.)*

RACHEL: Please. I need –

TOM: What? You need money again?

RACHEL: No –

TOM: Rach, I told you, I want to help you. But I can't keep giving you money. If Anna found out –

RACHEL: It's not about money.

TOM: You mentioned your landlord.

RACHEL: When?

TOM: One of your rambling messages. Saturday night. You were...

I thought you were going to stop drinking.

RACHEL: I'm sorry about the message.

TOM: You're always sorry.

They smile at each other.

RACHEL: I just want to know what happened.

TOM: I only know what Anna told me. You turned up at our house in a bit of a state. She said you threatened her.

RACHEL: That's not true.

TOM: Why would she lie?

RACHEL: She hates me. She wants you to hate me too.

TOM: She's frightened of you, Rach. She's actually scared of what you'll do next.

RACHEL: Because of that time with Evie?

I'd never hurt her, your baby. I'd never –

TOM: Wouldn't you?

RACHEL: No. You know that. You know me.

TOM: You once swung for me with a golf club.

RACHEL: I was drunk. I didn't know what I was doing.

TOM: That's what scares her. That's what scares me.

Beat.

RACHEL: So, Saturday, I argued with Anna, and then went home... Nothing else?

9

TOM: As far as I know. You'd gone when I came downstairs.

RACHEL: So, you weren't at the gym. And you didn't try to –

TOM: I didn't want any trouble.

RACHEL: So you got Anna to lie for you?

TOM: It wasn't like that.

    Beat.

RACHEL: Did I come back?

TOM: We didn't see you for the rest of the night.

RACHEL: I just keep getting the feeling I saw something. Or…

TOM: Where did you go once you left ours?

RACHEL: The off-licence. I ended up with this –

TOM: Did someone hurt you?

    TOM looks at the cut on her head. Touches it, tenderly.

TOM: Who was it?

RACHEL: I don't know.

TOM: You see, this was always the trouble.

RACHEL: What?

TOM: It was the same when we were married. You'd get drunk, and wake up with no memory of what you'd done.

    You were so different when you were sober.

RACHEL: I only began to drink when, when you and I…

TOM: Neither of us handled it brilliantly. I know that.

RACHEL: If we'd had a baby –

TOM: Don't do this to yourself, Rach. You can't live in some fantasy of the past.

RACHEL: But that's the thing with divorce. If someone dies, there's an ending. They're buried, there's a buffet, and then they're gone.

    I still have the loss, but with the knowing you're still out there. With the woman you were sleeping with when you were meant to be married to me.

TOM: I can't *keep* apologising.

(Puts his hand on her arm.) You deserve to be happy. If you just stopped drinking –

RACHEL: I haven't had a drink for two days.

TOM: You see? You can start again. Find your own…purpose.

Sorry. That sounds really patronising –

RACHEL: No, I know, I am trying. But…

TOM: But?

RACHEL: That detective…

TOM: Don't worry about him. He was asking me questions, and Anna as well.

RACHEL: But he doesn't believe me.

TOM: I believe you. Just tell him what you saw and let the police deal with it.

Rach… Please don't tell Anna that we've spoken like this.

RACHEL suddenly remembers something.

TOM: What?

MEGAN *appears, holds out her hand to someone, though we can't see to whom.*

RACHEL: I remember something.

Darkness. The sound of a train.

SCENE THREE

RACHEL enters with an array of newspapers. She scatters them on the floor and begins cutting out Megan Hipwell stories and pinning them to a wall. The photograph of MEGAN is pinned up, along with GASKILL's card. RACHEL accidentally cuts her finger.

RACHEL: Shit. *(Sucks the blood.)*

There's someone at the door. RACHEL hides everything.

GASKILL enters.

RACHEL: You got my message…

GASKILL: Surprised to hear from you. I got the feeling you were glad to see the back of – Oh, you've tidied.

RACHEL: *(Nervous.)* Oh, yeah. It's just that, well, sometimes, little things can trigger my memory.

GASKILL: Oh, I know that feeling. One minute I'm counting the stab wounds in a victim's stomach and then all of a sudden *(snaps his finger)* I remember I need to buy a new pair of oven gloves.

My wife used to take care of that sort of thing.

RACHEL: Divorced?

GASKILL: Heartbreak hotel with us two, isn't it? So, what did you remember?

RACHEL: *(Lying.)* I was…on the train, coming home from work and something suddenly came to me.

GASKILL: What did?

RACHEL: The line goes right past my old house – Blenheim Road. Well, it usually stops at the signal. It's not that I…but, you would, wouldn't you? You can't help but look back at the house you used to live in.

GASKILL: And you saw something? In your old house?

RACHEL: Do you want a drink? A soft drink, I mean.

GASKILL: Rachel. I don't have time to waste. Have you seen what the papers are saying?

RACHEL: *(Lying.)* No.

GASKILL: What d'you need to tell me?

RACHEL: It was Friday, the day before Megan went missing. I saw her, I saw her kissing someone.

GASKILL: In your old house?

RACHEL: No! No, I – I sometimes see her out the back of *her* house – a couple of doors down. They have this kind of terrace.

GASKILL becoming suspicious.

RACHEL: I'd see her out there, reading, drinking wine.

GASKILL: So, when I came here last time, and I asked if you knew Megan Hipwell, you weren't telling the truth?

RACHEL: I was telling you the truth, I just didn't realise I was lying.

Look, sorry! I see her. All the time, I see her – and her husband. They just look so…all of the time, they look so happy.

MEGAN and her husband, SCOTT, appear. They are dressing to go out. He zips up her dress. She untucks his shirt/roughs him up a little. Intimate. This continues while:

GASKILL: And you watch them?

RACHEL: Only when the train – Look, I don't know who she is – really, I don't. *(Embarrassed.)* I called her Jess, him Jason, in my mind.

GASKILL: A fantasy.

RACHEL: Don't you ever allow your imagination to wander? Don't you ever see someone and think, if I could step out of my shoes and into theirs, just for a day…

GASKILL: But you don't actually know who she is?

MEGAN and SCOTT disappear.

RACHEL: No. I imagined she was a stylist, or a photographer. And her husband, perhaps a doctor or an architect. Something exciting.

GASKILL: And where do you work?

RACHEL: In London.

GASKILL: Never heard of it.

RACHEL: *(Smiles.)* I'm in marketing.

GASKILL: The commute. The nine-to-five.

I've always been envious of commuters. It's the trains. I've always loved trains.

RACHEL: It's one of the things I didn't know I'd miss about my old life. The sound of the trains going past the house at night.

GASKILL: We used to sit on the banks and watch them as kids. Put apples and conkers on the tracks and watch them explode when the train ran over them. Scary, isn't it, that speed of a passing train?

RACHEL: I read that a train can rip the clothes right off you when it hits. It's not that uncommon, you know. Death by train.

GASKILL: So, Megan Hipwell – from your commuter train, you watch her going about her life. And – and let's just pretend there's nothing weird about that for a minute – when you last saw her, she was kissing someone. Her husband?

RACHEL: That's what I wanted to tell you. It wasn't her husband.

MEGAN appears. We see her, as before. MEGAN holding out her hand to someone.

A man appears. Not SCOTT. KAMAL ABDIC. He takes her hand. He embraces her. Kisses her. He kisses her again.

RACHEL: He was maybe Asian descent. Good-looking.

MEGAN and KAMAL disappear.

GASKILL: You've never seen this man before?

RACHEL: I don't think so.

GASKILL: Not in Megan's house? Not your old house?

RACHEL: No.

GASKILL: So, just to clarify. Every day, on your way to work, you go past the back of your old house, upon which you spy – as a matter of routine –

RACHEL: Well, not spy exactly –

GASKILL: And two doors down there's a woman whose life you consider to be enviable, and you spy on her too. You've given her a name and created a life for her – in your head. And now this woman has gone missing, your sketchy memory has suddenly conjured a man – who just happens to be tall, dark and handsome – and he was there the day before she vanished –

RACHEL: Look, I'd forgotten. I'd had a couple of drinks that morning –

GASKILL: You see, sometimes these cases attract a certain type of person.

RACHEL: No –

GASKILL: The kind of person who isn't above creating fantasies. Do you see where I'm going? Because if you don't, I'll talk you through it. Your life of nine-to-five, drinking alone, failed marriage – it's made you desperate to be a part of another life. One more 'exciting', as you put it –

RACHEL: That's not fair. I can help. I saw what was going on before you or anybody else even –

GASKILL: I'm gonna have to take all this down officially –

RACHEL: I see her at her most unguarded –

GASKILL: Unless I'm just wasting paper –

RACHEL: I'm just trying to tell you what I saw!

GASKILL: But, Rachel, you can't remember what you saw. Can you?

Darkness. The sound of the train screaming past.

SCENE FOUR

SCOTT and MEGAN HIPWELL's home. There's a painting on the wall.

SCOTT: You're another reporter, aren't you? I told your mate –

RACHEL: No! I'm not a / reporter – *(All overlapping.)*

SCOTT: / I'm not interested in the papers. I don't read them. Don't want to be / in them.

RACHEL: / No, Scott!

I'm a friend.

SCOTT: That's what the last guy said –

RACHEL: A friend of Megan's.

SCOTT appraises her.

SCOTT: I've never seen you before.

RACHEL: I'm Rachel. I used to go to Megan's art gallery. On Roseberry Avenue.

SCOTT: You're a collector? An artist?

RACHEL: *(Gestures a painting motion with a paintbrush.)* I dabble…

SCOTT: Looks like you're painting a shed.

Beat.

RACHEL: I am.

They smile.

SCOTT: Sorry. It's just been so… It's hard to know who to trust.

RACHEL: I'm just a friend. Nothing more. *(Lying, thinking on her feet.)* Megan and I would meet for coffee when she used to look after Evie.

SCOTT allows her in.

RACHEL: Oh, I love that smell. Always feels like a fresh start, doesn't it?

SCOTT: What smell?

RACHEL: You've just cleaned.

SCOTT: Have you heard from her?

RACHEL: I wish I had. I'm so sorry.

I didn't want to trouble you. But, for Megan's sake…

SCOTT: You know, it's amazing. It's only in the last few days I realised just how few friends Megan has.

RACHEL: Well, I think people like her, she's just quite…distant.

SCOTT: Does she ever talk about me?

RACHEL: We mostly speak about art.

SCOTT: That's one of the things we *don't* talk about.

RACHEL: No?

SCOTT: She gets frustrated trying to explain… Never mind.

RACHEL: How are the police getting on?

SCOTT: Useless. First there was this Riley woman. Everything she asked, like I'm on trial, you know? 'Did you and Megan argue much?' Well, we're not the fucking Waltons. And now this Gaskill fella. Says he's trying to speak to anyone who was in the area on Saturday. Well, that could take all year.

RACHEL: And was there anyone? Out of the ordinary, I mean.

SCOTT: I don't know any more than they've reported in the papers.

RACHEL: I didn't think you – sorry.

SCOTT: What?

RACHEL: I thought you said you don't read the papers. Sorry. I wasn't trying to say… So they haven't asked you about the possibility of…another man?

SCOTT: Are you saying she ran off with someone?

RACHEL: No. God, no! I just…

SCOTT: Is that where she's gone?

RACHEL: She never said anything to me. But, there was something I should tell you.

SCOTT gets himself a drink. Drinks. Remembers his manners.

SCOTT: Sorry. D'you want one?

She hesitates. He gives her a drink. She hesitates. Drinks.

SCOTT: I know what Megan's like. What I mean is, I know that there'll always be things about Megan I don't know. Her past. Did she ever show you this?

He gestures to the painting.

RACHEL: I don't think she did show me that one, no –

SCOTT: You've not been here before? Our house.

RACHEL: No. *(Looks around, trying to conceal what's almost excitement.) (Almost to herself.)* It's just how I imagined it.

SCOTT: It's one of Megan's. She did a few like this one. The same theme.

MEGAN *appears with SCOTT.*

MEGAN: *(Enthusiastic, passionate.)* **It's all about the bit that's missing. Don't you see?**

SCOTT: **I can see, but –**

MEGAN: **Look, here we have colour and light; and here there's a kind of drama, something wild, but no matter how much you try to focus on what's there, the eye is always drawn to what's absent.**

SCOTT: **Yeah, but what's it supposed to be?**

MEGAN: **Come on, Scott. Please try. Don't you ever feel that, that something of you is missing and the more you try to ignore it, the bigger the void gets?**

SCOTT: **So, what should be there?**

MEGAN: **That's the point! Only you know what should be there. There are voids like this in everyone. We try to exist around them but all the time, their gravity's trying to suck you in, like a black hole.**

MEGAN *disappears.*

SCOTT: I always tried to understand her art. But, Christ, when they have those exhibition parties, I always get stuck with some artist while they yabber on about the subtleties and subtexts of a painting – I just want to say 'what the fuck is it?'

So, you've tried calling her?

RACHEL: …

SCOTT: You've got her number?

RACHEL: *(Lying.)* Of course. It's just that, well, I dropped my phone. Sunday. I dropped it…in the toilet and I'm on this replacement. So, all my numbers have gone.

SCOTT: Here…

SCOTT dials the number on RACHEL's phone. We hear the ringing, until:

MEGAN: *(Recorded message.)* You've reached Megan Hipwell's phone. You know what to do.

RACHEL hangs up.

RACHEL: At least it's ringing.

SCOTT: What was it you wanted to tell me?

RACHEL: Scott. The thing is –

Someone at the door. GASKILL. Surprised to see RACHEL, drinking with SCOTT. Are they in on it together?

GASKILL: Sorry to – Oh. I didn't realise you had…

SCOTT: This is Rachel. She knew Megan from the art gallery.

GASKILL: *(Choosing to play along.)* From the art gallery…

I had some information. Probably not reliable. I'm not sure this is the best time to talk –

SCOTT: No. It's fine. Rachel's one of Megan's friends. Just say your piece.

A moment between GASKILL and RACHEL.

GASKILL: Well, strange as it might sound. Someone is convinced that they saw something in your home a couple of days before you reported Megan missing. The Friday.

SCOTT: What? What did they see?

GASKILL: This person said that from the train that passes by your house, they saw Megan with another man. *(Dryly.)* Dark and handsome.

SCOTT: From the train?

GASKILL: My hunch is that the person is someone who's seen the case on the news and wants to get themselves involved.

SCOTT: You don't believe it then?

GASKILL: I'd need to see a bit more evidence before I took that person too seriously.

SCOTT: So why are we even talking about it?

GASKILL: I have to follow these things up just in case. But, if you don't know another man in Megan's life…? Asian, perhaps…?

SCOTT: No.

GASKILL: Then, I'll leave you two in peace. For now.

It's good that you're getting support from your friends.

SCOTT: Rachel's Megan's friend really.

GASKILL: Ah. Well, I'll let you know if anything comes up. Otherwise, keep your phone on and stay vigilant.

SCOTT: Vigilant?

GASKILL: Just in case. There might be someone worming around in your life.

GASKILL leaves.

SCOTT: The fuck? Who watches someone's house from the train?

RACHEL: Could I have another drink?

SCOTT: Sure.

SCOTT fetches another couple of beers.

RACHEL: So, somebody saw Megan with another man…so who do you think this guy is?

SCOTT: I told you, she hardly had any friends. Just Tara and – I didn't even know about *you.*

RACHEL: Then isn't it possible that you didn't know about the other man?

SCOTT: Are you saying she did say something to you –

RACHEL: No! I just really think you should take it seriously.

SCOTT: …?

RACHEL: Don't you? You have a witness who said she saw something…

SCOTT: She? Did he say it was a she?

RACHEL: I think so, yes, but –

SCOTT: You don't know what it's been like. That reporter at the door, trying to get in and have a good old poke around.

He didn't say it was a she. He didn't –

Are you on the level? *Are* you a reporter?

RACHEL: No. I told you I'm –

SCOTT: Megan's friend. Who I've never heard of.

RACHEL: Please. I just wanted to talk to you –

SCOTT grabs RACHEL by the wrist, begins to lead RACHEL out.

SCOTT: I can't believe I was so –

RACHEL: No! Please!

SCOTT: Fucking reporters, trying to –

RACHEL: It was me!

Beat.

RACHEL: *I* saw it.

SCOTT lets her go. A stand-off. RACHEL nurses her wrist.

RACHEL: That's what I came to tell you, because Gaskill doesn't believe me. You saw that. But how could I live with myself if I didn't tell you?

The thing is – *(Points.)* That's the train I catch, to work. And sometimes I see Megan on your terrace.

SCOTT: And you saw her with another man? What, fucking?

RACHEL: No, they weren't…it was just kissing.

SCOTT: Who was it?

RACHEL: I don't know. That's why I thought –

SCOTT: Fucking brilliant…

RACHEL: That's why I thought, if I came and told you, perhaps you would know who it is. I'm trying to help. Really.

I've never seen him before. He was Asian though, I think.

SCOTT suddenly thinks of something. Starts looking in drawers. Retrieves a business card.

SCOTT: Kamal Abdic. Her therapist.

RACHEL: Is he Asian?

SCOTT: Kamal Abdic. He's not from the Cotswolds, is he?

RACHEL: She was in therapy?

SCOTT: She didn't tell you? I thought that was the sort of thing women were always banging on about. Sitting in Costa in your pilates kit, drinking skinny lattes and comparing anti-depressants.

RACHEL: She was private about things like –

Can I see this?

RACHEL takes the card. When the moment is right, she pockets it.

RACHEL: If she was seeing a therapist – maybe she was really unhappy.

SCOTT: Suicidal?

RACHEL: No. I'm just – can you think of any reason she might have run away?

SCOTT: … Look, I've got stuff to do –

RACHEL: The police don't believe me. If you tell them she was seeing this man, they'll look into it. They'll have to.

Here's my telephone number.

SCOTT doesn't take it.

RACHEL: I'll leave it here.

Tell the police about him. Tell them about Kamal Abdic.

RACHEL goes to leave. Turns back. Picks up her drink. Leaves with it. A big night's drinking ahead.

SCENE FIVE

RACHEL's evidence wall now has the addition of KAMAL ABDIC's business card and a very crude drawing of MEGAN's piece of art.

RACHEL takes some headache tablets with water. She turns on her phone. It beeps twice. She puts it on loudspeaker, listens to her messages.

ESTATE AGENT: Ah, Rachel Watson, this is Cathy from Newall's Estate Agents –

Message deleted.

SECRETARY: Hello, this is a message for Rachel Watson. I'm just returning your message from last night –

RACHEL: What?

SECRETARY: *(Continuing.)* As it happens, Dr Abdic has had a cancellation, so he's held a slot for you at eleven this morning. Do call back if you no longer want the appointment.

End of messages.

RACHEL: Shit.

RACHEL looks at her phone. An opportunity.

SCENE SIX

KAMAL ABDIC in his therapist's chair. RACHEL sits opposite. There's a painting on the wall, similar in theme to the one at MEGAN and SCOTT's place.

RACHEL: It's the best way I can describe it, like they get sucked into a black hole. And then, even the bits that remain are so fragmented, it's like…have you ever bought a jigsaw puzzle from a jumble sale? Bits missing and bits from other puzzles finding their way in. Does that make any sense?

KAMAL: You're saying the problem is not just what you have forgotten – what you remember is also –

RACHEL: Yes! I don't trust it. I don't trust my own memory not to trick me.

KAMAL: Why not?

RACHEL: I get these… I don't know, flashes of memory, but it's like, like I've tried to fit the wrong pieces into the puzzle. Tried to force bits in just to complete the picture.

KAMAL: When did this start?

RACHEL: *(Smiles.)* I don't remember.

KAMAL: What are the black holes?

RACHEL: So…at the weekend I woke up with this. *(Points to her head.)* No idea how it got there. And then, someone says something, and I'll almost see it. The memory. But it's always…the more I try to reach for it, the further I push it away.

KAMAL: And what can you remember from the weekend?

RACHEL: I was in an underpass. I felt this blow to my head. That's all.

KAMAL: Could it be that the blow to your head is the reason in itself that you can't remember?

RACHEL: No. It happens all the time. That's why I hoped there might be some techniques you could give me. But then…

KAMAL: But then?

RACHEL: I don't know. I suppose… Maybe, maybe I'm afraid.

KAMAL: Of what you did?

RACHEL: And not just that night. All the awful things I've ever done.

KAMAL: You must have a very low opinion of yourself.

RACHEL: Why?

KAMAL: You have periods of memory loss, and you assume that the blank spaces are filled with you doing something awful or embarrassing. Why not something kind or funny or intelligent?

Are you capable of kindness? Humour? Intelligence?

RACHEL: Yes.

KAMAL: So, where are those puzzle pieces?

RACHEL: I just want to remember what happened Saturday night.

KAMAL: Why is that night so important?

RACHEL: Saturday night. It was cold. Do you remember?

KAMAL: (*Gently.*) The power over memory is yours. Okay, if you have a neurological condition, then your issue is a medical one. If not, then it's psychological. Which means it's back in your hands.

RACHEL: But my memory tells me one thing and then evidence tells me something else. There was one time, when I was married, I got so enraged with my husband –

TOM appears.

TOM: **Rach. Rachel, please. Put it down. Put it down, now. You're scaring me.**

RACHEL swings a golf club at TOM. TOM ducking each time.

TOM: **Don't do this again, Rachel. This isn't you.**

You have to control it, before you really hurt someone.

RACHEL swings again, wildly, violently. We hear a loud smash.

Turns back to KAMAL.

RACHEL: This strength, it just comes from somewhere.

I don't remember doing it, but I took out a massive chunk of the wall. It's there for all to see, what I'd done.

KAMAL: So, rage. Violence. Anger.

RACHEL: That's not who I am. I know I'm not.

It was easier when I was with my husband. He was always there –

RACHEL turns to look at where he was. But he's gone.

RACHEL: To pick up the pieces.

KAMAL: Violence clouds the memory. And then you have to reconstruct it. Only, now the memory is susceptible to other influences. Do you understand? Sometimes we're able to manipulate our own history by reshaping a memory. Or we cherry-pick the memories we like, or repress the ones we don't.

RACHEL: Your voice. It's very…gentle.

Is that your real voice or just for…this?

Beat.

RACHEL: You don't ever get to know your clients personally? Become…friends.

KAMAL: You were talking about your ex-husband.

RACHEL: Tom. Yes. He always used to take my side.

KAMAL: And he's still a fixture, it seems. Emotionally.

RACHEL: He'd still be a fixture physically, if we'd have been able to have a baby.

We tried. Tried for years. Did the IVF. Spent a fortune. We even tried the alternative therapies, you know? Reflexology, acupuncture, crystal therapy.

KAMAL: Crystal therapy?

RACHEL: You sort of lie there and someone puts glass beads on your forehead and plays the sounds of the ocean.

KAMAL: And even that didn't get you pregnant?

RACHEL: I know. *(Smiles.)* Ovaries of stone.

KAMAL: And this affected your marriage?

RACHEL: As soon as we began talking about having a family,
and…it was my fault. Physically. My fault we couldn't…
All that time, I lived with this empty space, here, where our
child should have been. Just hoping.

RACHEL looks at the picture again. KAMAL notices.

RACHEL: It's sort of about what *isn't* there, don't you think?

KAMAL suspicious of what RACHEL is saying. Continues.

KAMAL: If your problem was physiological, then I can't accept
that it was your fault. Surely, it's beyond your control.

RACHEL: If we'd had Evie – a baby, if we'd had a baby, we'd
still be together.

KAMAL: *(Smiles.)* Okay. And I think you know my next
question…

RACHEL: Tom and his new wife, Anna, they have a baby. Evie.

Anna posted a picture on Facebook, when Evie was born.
The three of them, a *selfie*, in hospital. She wrote, 'So that's
what all the fuss is about! Never known love like this.
Happiest day of our lives.'

She knew I'd see.

KAMAL: And how did that –

RACHEL: I wanted to smash her head in. To grab her hair
and…sorry.

Embarrassed moment.

KAMAL: Everyone has bad thoughts. It's how we act on them
that counts.

RACHEL: Do you? Have bad thoughts?

KAMAL: It's impossible to be kind in your head, all the time.

RACHEL: And do you act on them?

KAMAL: So, there we have Tom and his new wife and baby. And what's Rachel doing?

RACHEL: We still love each other. I know we do. It doesn't even feel like we're really divorced, because…

RACHEL shifts a gear.

RACHEL: It's more like he's gone missing. You know, like that woman who's just gone missing?

KAMAL doesn't commit to a response.

RACHEL: You must have heard. Megan Hipwell. She's been missing since Saturday.

KAMAL: Yes. I think I saw something on the news.

RACHEL: You don't know her?

KAMAL: No.

RACHEL: But that can't be right. It was Megan who gave me your number. She's one of your clients.

KAMAL: You know Megan?

RACHEL: Probably not as well as you do.

So…?

KAMAL: We have a client confidentiality policy here. I can't go around –

RACHEL: Have the police spoken to you yet?

KAMAL: Why would they –

RACHEL: But you do know that she's missing?

KAMAL: This is meant to be about you.

RACHEL: What do you think's happened to her?

KAMAL: I've no idea –

RACHEL: But she must open up to you –

KAMAL: I really can't disclose –

RACHEL: They're talking about another man. Did she ever mention another man to you?

KAMAL: What would it matter if she did?

RACHEL: So she did mention another man!

KAMAL: No, of course not –

RACHEL: Why 'of course not'? She's a beautiful woman. Isn't it possible that she has another man? Surely that's the kind of thing she would have spoken to you about?

KAMAL: No.

RACHEL: So, what does she talk to you about?

KAMAL: Look. I'd lose my job if I broke our confidentiality policy.

RACHEL stands. Looks at the painting on the wall.

RACHEL: I like this painting. I guess, there are voids like this in everyone. We try to fill them, we try to exist around them but all the time their gravity's sucking you in, like a black hole.

They look at each other. KAMAL knows he's been rumbled.

RACHEL: Wouldn't it be in conflict with professional boundaries to accept gifts from a client?

KAMAL: That's not what –

RACHEL: Did she give it to you as a friend, then?

Beat.

RACHEL: Does she have another man in her life?

KAMAL: No. You don't understand.

RACHEL: So, the only other man she speaks to, other than her husband, is you –

KAMAL: You can't back me into a corner like this –

RACHEL: What do I do when the police ask me about any other men in her life?

Perhaps I'll just tell Detective Gaskill to come directly to you.

RACHEL takes out her phone. KAMAL stops her from making the call.

KAMAL: All right. All right there was someone.

(*Taking her into his confidence.*) I'm only telling you this because you're her friend.

29

RACHEL: Who was he?

MEGAN appears.

MEGAN: Someone I used to know. I Googled him, just to see. I forgot to delete my browser history.

KAMAL: Does Scott check your internet history?

MEGAN: He doesn't trust me, I suppose. He's right not to. He wanted to know who this guy was. I told him, he was just a friend from the past. He wanted to know all about him, but I couldn't say.

KAMAL: Why? Are you afraid of Scott?

MEGAN: Of course not. He's my husband.

KAMAL: Reading your emails. Going through your internet history. It's a form of emotional abuse.

MEGAN: It isn't abuse. Not if you deserve it.

KAMAL: Why would you deserve it?

Back to the present.

RACHEL: So, who was this guy?

KAMAL: Why are you here?

RACHEL: Why haven't you told the police what you know?

KAMAL: There's nothing to tell.

RACHEL: Who was he?

Back to MEGAN and KAMAL.

MEGAN: Craig McKenzie. The first man I ever loved. After Ben died, and I ran away –

KAMAL: Who's Ben?

MEGAN: My brother. We were going to go to America, but we never made it. Ben didn't make it anywhere. He died in a motorcycle accident. On the A10. Near a place called Buntingford. Who dies near a place called Buntingford? Not even in Buntingford. Just near it.

When I die, I want to be near the sea. No need for a ceremony, no gravestone. Just to be in the right place, to have my own ending.

Anyway, I ran away, got into some trouble. I was arrested, for...

KAMAL: For?

MEGAN: Soliciting. I was fifteen. Then I met Craig McKenzie. He saved me. For a while, at least.

KAMAL: But he's no longer around? What happened there?

MEGAN: ... I don't think I'm ready to talk about that yet.

Back to the present.

RACHEL: So, has she run away to look for this guy?

KAMAL: I don't know.

RACHEL: When did you last see her?

KAMAL: She had an appointment, a week ago on Wednesday.

RACHEL: And then she disappeared on the Saturday. You didn't see her in between.

KAMAL: No.

RACHEL: Are you sure?

KAMAL: *(Getting angry.)* Yes, I'm sure.

RACHEL: So the gentle voice *is* just for –

KAMAL: Listen. I've nothing more to say about Megan Hipwell. She's my client. I saw her on Wednesday for her appointment, and I haven't seen her since.

RACHEL: Well, that's funny, because I saw you with her on Friday morning.

KAMAL: ...

RACHEL: I saw you kissing her. On their terrace.

A stand-off.

KAMAL: I think you should leave.

RACHEL: I hear that a lot. I need to go to the police.

KAMAL physically stops her. He holds her tightly by the arm.

KAMAL: I would not hurt her.

RACHEL: Where is she?

KAMAL: I haven't seen her since Friday.

RACHEL: So it *was* you kissing her.

And you haven't told the police.

KAMAL: I'd lose my job.

And they'd think –

RACHEL: What would they think?

KAMAL: I'd never hurt anyone. I'm not –

RACHEL: Violent?

Beat.

KAMAL lets go of her arm.

RACHEL: So where is she then? Should the police search here? Search your house?

KAMAL: No! She's… She's probably run away.

RACHEL: Why?

KAMAL: I can't tell you.

RACHEL: Because it implicates you?

KAMAL: Because I'm bound by my profession.

RACHEL: Not so bound, it seems. Where? Where would she run to?

Silence.

RACHEL: If you know something, you have to say. Or don't you want them to find her?

What makes you think she ran away?

Back to MEGAN.

MEGAN: **Sometimes I just sit with my eyes closed and listen to the trains rumble past. The idea of getting away, somewhere, anywhere.**

KAMAL: Is there a destination?

MEGAN: There's a little seaside town in Norfolk. Holkham. It's weird that I still think of it with such affection, such longing, but I do. The mice-infested house, full of candles and dirt and music.

KAMAL: Why this particular house?

MEGAN: Just some place I seem to remember. I don't know.

KAMAL: You close your eyes and you run away to this place.

MEGAN: If only in my mind.

My art teacher at school, he said I was a mistress of reinvention. I loved the idea. Each day, be someone new. Just hop a train and start again. Be a stranger. I suppose he just wanted to fuck me.

But sometimes, I can't sleep because of it. Can't draw. Can't paint. The urge to run overwhelms me. At night, when I lie awake I can hear it. A whisper in my head saying, 'slip away'.

There's something I have to tell Scott. And when I do...

Perhaps it's better I just leave.

RACHEL brings us back to the present.

RACHEL: So, she ran away! But, that's good, isn't it? You have to tell the police.

KAMAL: They're doing their job, I'm doing mine.

RACHEL: *(Going to leave.)* Then I'll tell them.

KAMAL: Rachel... You don't have to get involved.

RACHEL: I am involved.

The sound of a train crashing past.

SCENE SEVEN

Police station. Two chairs, in which neither RACHEL nor GASKILL sit.

RACHEL: There's something you need to know –

GASKILL: More bits emerging from that mysterious memory of yours?

RACHEL: I came here to help you.

GASKILL: And what a reliable source of help you've been so far.

RACHEL: You need to write this down.

GASKILL: And waste more paper?

RACHEL: No –

GASKILL: More police time

RACHEL: I'm trying to –

GASKILL: When we first met, in your flat, I felt sorry for you. I genuinely did. The eviction notice, the pint-sized version of alcoholism –

RACHEL: I don't want pity –

GASKILL: And then this obsession with your ex-husband, and his neighbours –

RACHEL: I'm not here to be humiliated –

GASKILL: But at every step of the investigation, I hear the name Rachel Watson. Or, as with last night, I bump into you at the scene of the crime.

RACHEL: Has a crime been committed?

GASKILL: So I have to ask myself. Who *is* Rachel Watson? *(Takes out his notepad.)*

RACHEL: I was at Scott Hipwell's to tell him what you refuse to believe.

GASKILL: The handsome stranger.

RACHEL: You're so behind.

GASKILL: First, I think we need to establish, for the record, whether you actually know Megan Hipwell or not.

34

RACHEL: If you'd just listen to what I've been saying –

GASKILL: The next time my superintendent asks me if I have any suspects, would you blame me for mentioning one Rachel Watson, a half-cut, violent fantasist who's obsessed with the missing woman. One Rachel Watson, who, on the night Megan went missing, was seen in the neighbourhood, and what's her alibi? Black holes in her memory. Which is no alibi at all.

RACHEL: Look. I don't actually know Megan, other than spying on her from the – not spying. Don't write that!

GASKILL: I *am* writing that.

You see, the trouble with fantasists, as with liars, they have to keep lying to justify what they've already made up. Just to stay in the game.

RACHEL: How can I make you see that I'm not making this up? You're a buffoon.

You can write that.

GASKILL: I'm not writing that. You see, there's a theory building, isn't there? You wanted the life of Megan Hipwell. To achieve that, you had to get her out of the way. Perhaps it was always a fantasy but, when you saw Megan's supposed infidelity, you saw it as a chance to swoop, to get close to Scott Hipwell. Something you seem to have achieved.

RACHEL: No.

GASKILL: I think you need to give me one good reason why I shouldn't arrest you.

RACHEL: You can't arrest me. I'm going to arrest you!

GASKILL: Give me a reason.

RACHEL: She's in Norfolk.

Beat.

GASKILL: What do you know that you haven't been telling me?

RACHEL: I'm telling you everything I know. You just refuse to listen –

35

GASKILL: How do you know she's in Norfolk?

RACHEL: Megan fantasised about running away. She had a vision of a rundown house in a seaside town there.

GASKILL: And she told you this? No! No, she didn't tell you this. Because you never met her. Not even once.

RACHEL: Have you looked in Norfolk?

GASKILL: How come you've only just thought to mention this? Where did you get this idea from?

Where did it come from?

RACHEL: … *(Lying.)* Scott.

GASKILL: Scott Hipwell told you that Megan wanted to run away to Norfolk, but he didn't think to tell *us* that's where she might be? Didn't think to go himself for a little look-see.

RACHEL: The point is, we know where she's gone.

GASKILL: What about our tall, dark handsome bugger? Has he –

GASKILL notices something. The bruises on her wrists.

GASKILL: Has he gone now?

RACHEL: I don't know. I don't know how he fits in anymore.

GASKILL: Do you want a drink? A soft drink, I mean. Tea or something.

RACHEL: No.

Beat.

GASKILL: What's all this? *(He takes RACHEL's wrists.)* Bruises.

How did you get these? No more lies.

RACHEL: … Scott. He thought I was a reporter. That I'd tried to trick my way into his house.

GASKILL: Rachel, I was there. Remember? He wasn't dragging you out. You were getting drunk together.

RACHEL: I was there, doing your job. You wonder why you keep bumping into me – it's because I'm always a step ahead.

GASKILL: Scott, then. Violent towards women. That's what I'm to glean from this conversation. Right?

RACHEL: I didn't say that.

GASKILL: You said he caused these bruises on you. Is that not violent?

Did you notice how clean his house smelt? Bleach and all that flowery stuff.

Does he strike you as the housemaid type, Scott Hipwell? Prancing around in his marigolds, doing the old shake and vac?

RACHEL: He hasn't hurt his wife.

GASKILL: I spoke with him this morning.

RACHEL: And...?

GASKILL: He told me about Megan's therapist –

RACHEL: Forget the therapist. You need to go to Norfolk. Find a guy called Craig McKenzie.

GASKILL: Who's Craig McKenzie?

RACHEL: Megan lived with him in a place called Holkham.

GASKILL: How could you know this, if you didn't know Megan?

RACHEL: I bet she's there with him. You have to find him. Find Craig McKenzie.

RACHEL's phone rings. She looks at it. Unknown number. She hesitates, decides to answer.

RACHEL: Hello?

Sound of a train crashing by.

SCENE EIGHT

RACHEL at SCOTT's.

SCOTT: You've heard what they're saying about her?

RACHEL: I'm sure it's not true.

SCOTT: Did she ever tell you about a baby? A baby who died.

RACHEL: Megan wouldn't kill a child. I know she wouldn't.

SCOTT: Who spreads bullshit like this?

RACHEL: *(Sympathetic.)* There are people out there. Fantasists. They'll make up anything, just to be involved.

SCOTT laughs wryly.

RACHEL: What?

SCOTT: That's what Gaskill said about you.

RACHEL: Have you and Gaskill been talking about me?

SCOTT: He said they're going to question that therapist.

RACHEL: That's good, isn't it? She'd tell him things she wouldn't tell anyone else.

What *did* Gaskill say about me?

SCOTT: D'you want a drink?

RACHEL: I don't drink. Not anymore.

SCOTT: Tea, or something. Sparkling water.

He gives her a bottle of Buxton sparking water. A bottle of lager for himself.

SCOTT: Tell me honestly. Are you really Megan's friend?

RACHEL: … It's more that our lives were sort of…aligned. I did know her, but –

SCOTT: Oh, my fucking… How stupid am I?

RACHEL: No. You're not. Please…let me explain.

SCOTT: How do you explain all this?

RACHEL: Look – I saw Megan, didn't I, the day before she disappeared. The police didn't believe me. I *knew* it mattered. But if I just said it, how it was –

SCOTT: That you spy on us from the train –

RACHEL: You'd think I was…that there's something wrong with me. I said I was her friend, so you'd let me help.

SCOTT: Help! Gaskill was asking me all about cleaning fluids and why I was suddenly so house-proud.

RACHEL: That was nothing to do with me.

SCOTT: What did you tell him?

RACHEL: I didn't say anything.

SCOTT: All you've done is lie.

RACHEL: But I haven't lied about what I saw. What would I have to gain?

SCOTT: To make your own life more exciting? Is your life really that shit?

RACHEL: *(Doesn't know whether to laugh or cry.)* My life is pretty shit, actually. Divorced. Childless. I've put on weight. My face has gone all puffy, like a chipmunk. I can't get over the fact that Tom (my ex-husband) betrayed me. I can't even pay my rent, so I'm about to be evicted. Everyone thinks I'm – at best, a stalker, at worst –

SCOTT: You don't even know Megan – do you?

Before RACHEL can answer, the doorbell rings.

Beat. SCOTT goes to the door. TOM and ANNA enter.

ANNA: We came to –

A look of horror on the faces of all but SCOTT, who is oblivious to the connection.

TOM: We just wanted to make sure you're doing okay… But you've got company, so [we'll leave you to it] –

SCOTT: Oh, sorry, this is Rachel. Tom and Anna. They live a couple of doors down.

RACHEL: Hello.

ANNA: *(Overlapping.)* Hello.

TOM: *(Overlapping.)* Hi.

Awkward silence.

TOM: *(Simultaneously.)* Well, we won't –

SCOTT: *(Simultaneously.)* Where's Evie?

TOM: Anna's mum has her for the night.

SCOTT: D'you want a drink?

TOM: We don't want to intrude. We just brought you some…
    (Gestures to food and drink.)

SCOTT: No, that's brilliant. Cheers.

ANNA: It's Moroccan chicken, with lemon couscous. Nothing
    fancy. The chicken's organic.

SCOTT: Sounds great. Thanks.

Awkward.

ANNA: And the wine, it's… *(ANNA reads the label.)* –

RACHEL: White.

ANNA: From the Marlborough region.

SCOTT: Right. Thanks. I'll pour us all a glass.

    Well, not Rachel. She doesn't drink –

    TOM, ANNA and RACHEL share a glance. 'Rachel doesn't drink'!

RACHEL: Sparkling water. From the Buxton region.

TOM: We really don't want to –

ANNA: A drink would be lovely. Thank you.

    SCOTT opens the bottle, pours three glasses.

ANNA: So. How do you two know each other?

SCOTT: Rachel's helping in the search for Megan.

ANNA: Do you know something we don't?

RACHEL: Probably.

    Beat.

TOM: If there's anything we can do, mate…

RACHEL: Like what?

    They drink. Awkward.

SCOTT: How's Evie? She must be, what…four months?

ANNA: Six months.

SCOTT: Goes fast.

ANNA: She almost sleeps through, now.

RACHEL: Almost?

TOM: Sorry –

RACHEL: No, I'm just interested.

Beat.

ANNA: She wakes about four every morning. So I bring take her into our bed.

RACHEL: I suppose, the trouble with that, it creates a cycle of dependence.

ANNA: I'm sorry?

RACHEL: Well, if you always take her into *your* bed at that time, then she'll always wake up at that time, won't she?

ANNA: Do you have children, Rachel?

TOM: Scott. Mate. All of this, must be a complete headfuck.

SCOTT: Have you heard the latest?

TOM: …

SCOTT: You have.

RACHEL: I'm sure it's not true.

All eyes on RACHEL.

ANNA: Do you know Megan?

RACHEL: I know she wouldn't hurt a child.

ANNA: I suppose we never know what anyone's really capable of.

TOM: Look. It's nothing to do with us.

SCOTT: Must be weird, hearing your old babysitter might have killed a child.

TOM: Evie's fine. Megan was always great with Evie.

Prolonged awkward moment; no one knows what to say.

They sip their drinks.

Very awkward silence.

TOM downs his drink. ANNA follows suit.

TOM: Well, it's getting late. We'd better get back for Evie.

RACHEL: I thought you said, Anna's mum –

TOM: She was just passing.

(To SCOTT.) So, call us if there's anything at all. You know, we're just down the road.

SCOTT: Yeah. Cheers. Thanks for the chicken.

ANNA: It's organic.

TOM: I'm sure everything'll…just let us know if there's anything we can do.

Bye, Rachel.

RACHEL: Bye.

TOM and ANNA leave.

SCOTT: That was weird. The Watsons are normally –

Watson? Rachel Watson?

RACHEL: It is getting late. I really should be –

SCOTT: You said Tom. Earlier when you said about your ex-husband, you called him Tom.

RACHEL: … It didn't seem important.

SCOTT: I knew everyone was acting weird. Why didn't anyone say? And why didn't you ever mention that you're Tom's ex-wife?

RACHEL: That's got nothing to do with this –

SCOTT: Hasn't it?

Christ, one minute I'm just a normal bloke, with a wife and a mortgage. Now I'm a circus attraction. The reporters. The curtain-twitchers opposite. You. All getting off on my pain. I mean, for fuck's sake, they brought me chicken!

RACHEL: Weren't they just trying to be nice?

SCOTT: I'm a vegetarian. They're not thinking about me, they just want a front row seat.

RACHEL: … I'm sorry for everything that's happened. I won't bother you again.

RACHEL offers a handshake.

SCOTT: You don't look like a chipmunk.

RACHEL: Thanks.

Shared moment. RACHEL turns to go.

SCOTT: Rachel, there's something I…

RACHEL: What?

SCOTT: … I really do love her. I just want her to come home.

SCOTT tries not to cry. RACHEL holds him. The embrace goes on and on.

Suddenly, SCOTT's hand is on RACHEL's hair, her back. It's thrilling.

RACHEL pulls away.

SCOTT: Shit. I'm so sorry. That should never have –

Are you all right?

RACHEL: Yes. Sorry.

I shouldn't have come.

RACHEL goes to leave. Turns back.

RACHEL: Scott…

SCOTT: Yeah?

RACHEL: It doesn't matter.

SCOTT: You were gonna say it, just say it.

RACHEL: Why *were* you cleaning right after Megan went missing? It seems like you'd have bigger things to worry about.

SCOTT: It was a bird. A magpie had got trapped inside the house. It couldn't get out. It shat everywhere. Up the walls, the lot. I was just cleaning up.

RACHEL: What happened to the bird?

The sound of a train rumbling past.

SCENE NINE

RACHEL is listening to her messages:

MESSAGE 1: Rachel, this is Cathy from Newall's Estate Agents. You still haven't responded to our letters dated –

RACHEL presses delete.

MESSAGE 2: Miss Watson. Andrew Dayton here from Newall's. Can you contact us regarding your eviction –

Delete.

MESSAGE 3: Mike Newall here. Newall's Estate Agents –

Delete.

Knock at the door. GASKILL.

GASKILL: Well, this has been a funny old week, hasn't it?

GASKILL sees RACHEL's evidence wall.

GASKILL: *(Picks up the photo of MEGAN.)* So that's where my picture of Megan went. *(Picks up the KAMAL ABDIC business card.)* Yes, Scott said you must have taken that. *(Reading all the newspaper cuttings.)* We'll have to get you a scrap book for this lot. *(Picks up RACHEL's drawing.)* Modern art?

GASKILL: Funny, isn't it? The more bizarre your behaviour, the less I'm surprised by it.

(Sighs.) Usually when there's a development in a case, I get on the blower to my Super. But with this, it felt as if you're the one I need to update. What's all that about, I wonder?

RACHEL: And is there something?

GASKILL: Yes. I wanted to tell you that we've found her –

RACHEL: That's brilliant! Where? In Holkham?

GASKILL: No. No. Rachel, we've *found* her.

Darkness. The sound of a train and the screaming of magpies.

Act Two

SCENE ONE

Darkness. The sound of magpies chattering and calling. We hear a distant song sung by school children:

One for sorrow two for joy,

Three for a girl four a for a boy,

Five for silver six for gold,

Seven for a secret, never to be told.

Magpie, magpie why do you sigh,

I sit so alone while the world goes by.

This should repeat until the sound of a passing train sounds it out. The train fades into the distance. Lights up.

Police tape has been stretched around the area of wasteland where the pile of stones was. There is now a shallow grave. Two forensic officers in white overalls bag up things from the site.

GASKILL stands near the grave. RACHEL stands back.

GASKILL: Right. You wanted to know what happened to Megan Hipwell. There you go. Yards from her own home.

GASKILL trying to read RACHEL's reaction.

RACHEL: *(Gathering herself.)* Where've they taken her?

GASKILL: There'll be an autopsy.

RACHEL: How did she look?

A look from GASKILL. How d'you think she looked?

GASKILL: She'd had a blow to the head – same as you. Coincidence, I suppose.

RACHEL: I've never seen a dead body.

You must get to see it a lot, right? Is it really gory?

45

GASKILL: Nah, not always. Some fellas look better dead than they ever did alive. I'd never seen my poor old dad look so happy. Or maybe it was relief. Oh well.

RACHEL: Have you found anything here? Evidence, or...?

GASKILL: It's more what we haven't found. Megan was wearing a hat when she went missing. A grey beret. Very stylish. If we can locate that... But for now, my focus is on potential witnesses.

RACHEL: Surely there must be something here. That's what you do, isn't it? You find a dropped earring, or a torn piece of clothing, or – Isn't that what they're doing? *(Pointing to the forensic officers.)*

GASKILL: Yep. We've been up and down the tracks here all morning. I found a dead magpie just up the way there.

RACHEL momentarily surprised at the mention of magpies, again.

GASKILL: They have funerals for their dead, the magpies. Did you know that?

RACHEL: No.

GASKILL: One of the forensic lot told me. One magpie sees the dead one and calls a funeral song. Others come and join, apparently. A proper funeral.

RACHEL: Perhaps it's to do with survival...

GASKILL: What isn't?

RACHEL: And what about her handbag, her pockets, her phone, that sort of thing?

GASKILL: *(Not giving anything away.)* Let's get away from here.

GASKILL walks in the direction of the underpass. RACHEL hesitates, but follows.

GASKILL: Now, when I spoke to you last week, you were telling me about the black holes in your memory. Well, now you're one of my main...

RACHEL: Suspects!?

GASKILL: Witnesses. I need to see if we can step a little further into those black holes, clarify exactly what you saw that Saturday night. Here's the underpass you got your blow to your head, yes?

RACHEL suddenly uncomfortable without fully understanding why. She stares at the tunnel.

RACHEL: Can't we go somewhere else?

GASKILL suspicious.

GASKILL: Does being here bring anything back?

RACHEL: *(A moment of self-doubt.)* I…

GASKILL: Rachel?

RACHEL: I don't think it's as easy as that. And you don't believe anything I tell you anyway.

GASKILL: You were right about Kamal Abdic. Megan's DNA was all over his house. They were more than counsellor/client. He's admitted as much now. That was thanks to you.

RACHEL: Did you say 'thanks'?

GASKILL: Well…

RACHEL: You can say it again if you want.

GASKILL: You'd have to admit, your story was a little…

RACHEL: So what about the DNA?

GASKILL: All over the kitchen and the lounge.

RACHEL: And the bedroom?

GASKILL: *(Shaking his head, no.)* I was surprised by that.

RACHEL: I suppose you don't need a bed to have sex. Spur of the moment. Passionate.

GASKILL: I wouldn't remember.

Beat.

RACHEL: Neither would I.

A look between them. Sexual awkwardness.

RACHEL: So, hang on, Kamal had Megan at his house, and you've let him go?

GASKILL: It's not a crime to have someone in your kitchen.

RACHEL: The papers said he had a history of domestic violence.

GASKILL: The papers say a lot of things.

RACHEL: Like, 'Police incompetence'. 'No progress'. I saw the picture of you. You looked tired. Are you okay?

GASKILL: No. No. Don't. I'm not one of those TV detectives, who can't sleep until the case is solved. Once I get in my car to go home *(lights begin to change, as RACHEL is remembering something)* that's me for the – Rachel?

Lights take us back to RACHEL's memory:

RACHEL: Is someone there?

We see in the tunnel a figure. Neither RACHEL nor we can see who it is.

RACHEL: Hello?

ANNA: What are you doing?

RACHEL: *(Recognition.)* Is that you?

We see the figure more clearly. It is ANNA.

RACHEL: Anna?

ANNA disappears. The sound of a car door slamming. A car starting.

RACHEL: It was Anna I saw!

GASKILL: Anna Watson?

RACHEL: It was our old car. It has a little golf ball thing on the aerial. I bought it for Tom as a joke.

GASKILL: Does he play golf?

RACHEL: He hates it. He just plays to fit in.

GASKILL: So…it could have been Tom here.

RACHEL: Yeah, but –

GASKILL: *(Pulls out his notepad.)* He knew Megan, didn't he? I think Megan used to look after their little girl –

RACHEL: It was definitely a woman.

GASKILL: Do you think a woman could have killed Megan like that?

RACHEL: …

GASKILL: Do you?

RACHEL: I don't know.

GASKILL: And you think it was Anna Watson you saw. That she was the one who hit you?

RACHEL: That's not what I'm saying. But it was Anna, here. You have to talk to her.

GASKILL: Do you want to get back with Tom?

RACHEL: What?

GASKILL: If Anna Watson was out the way, you could get back with Tom.

RACHEL: But it's Megan who's been murdered.

GASKILL: If Anna was convicted of the murder…

RACHEL: I thought we were on the same side now. D'you really think I'd murder one woman to frame another?

GASKILL: Or is it Scott you like?

RACHEL: That I'd think any man is really worth killing for?

GASKILL: You could have the pick of two.

RACHEL: That's ridiculous.

GASKILL: Or is it three?

RACHEL: Who else?

GASKILL: Kamal Abdic.

RACHEL: I don't even know Kamal Abdic.

GASKILL: You've spied on him.

RACHEL: I've never met him.

GASKILL: Haven't you?

RACHEL: No.

GASKILL: *(Pulling a piece of paper from his pocket.)* Photocopied from his appointments diary. Friday. Eleven o'clock. Rachel Watson.

RACHEL: *(RACHEL takes the photocopy. It will later go on her evidence wall.)* I was just doing the work you wouldn't do. It was Kamal who told me about Megan's desire to run away. Have you even tried looking for this Craig McKenzie?

Pause.

GASKILL: *(Changing tack.)* Where do you work?

RACHEL: I told you.

GASKILL: You said London. The commute, but –

RACHEL: Huntingdon Whiteley.

GASKILL: *(Almost feeling sorry for her.)* Rachel, I checked.

RACHEL: No.

GASKILL: You haven't worked at Huntingdon Whiteley for six months.

RACHEL: You don't understand.

GASKILL: Every morning when you're watching the Watsons and the Hipwells from the train, you're not on your way to work. You take the train for the sole purpose of spying on them.

RACHEL: It's no one's business what I do. As you – and they – constantly remind me, I've nothing to do with any of their lives. Talk to Anna. Ask her why she was here.

RACHEL goes to leave.

GASKILL: Rachel. You asked about Megan's phone. If there were any clues.

RACHEL: Yeah?

GASKILL: The last call to her mobile phone – it was from you.

Darkness. The sound of a train screaming past.

SCENE TWO

RACHEL is hastily packing, deciding what to keep or chuck. The items convey a woman who has never been sure of her identity.

SCOTT appears.

SCOTT: Hey.

> *Beat.*

RACHEL: I'm so sorry about Megan.

> *RACHEL gives SCOTT a hug. Realises the awkwardness, quickly pulls away.*

SCOTT: I wanted to talk to you about –

> *SCOTT looks at RACHEL's evidence wall.*

SCOTT: Fucking… [hell]?

> *He picks out the photograph of MEGAN.*

SCOTT: Is this all part of your fantasy?

RACHEL: No! I wish everyone would stop saying –

SCOTT: It looks like a plan. Like you planned it all. Has Gaskill seen this?

RACHEL: Yes. He's seen it. He knows I was just trying to find her. You know that, too, right?

> *Beat.*

SCOTT: Looks like you're moving.

RACHEL: I'm having a clear out. Don't you ever need to do that? Just to make space in your head.

Sorry.

Have they told you anything? Have they got anyone?

SCOTT: Yeah, me!

RACHEL: What?

SCOTT: They've had me in for questioning. Again.

RACHEL: Why?

SCOTT: They wanted to ask me about Megan's mobile phone.

GASKILL appears. Back in time:

GASKILL: It was in her pocket.

SCOTT: What about it?

GASKILL: I don't want to take up more of your time than necessary. I know what you must be going through.

SCOTT: I doubt it.

GASKILL: Scott. There was a voicemail on Megan's phone. At 6.02pm, the night she disappeared.

SCOTT's voicemail plays.

SCOTT'S VOICE: I could kill you, you lying bitch.

SCOTT: ... We had a row. Neither of us are perfect. It didn't mean anything.

GASKILL: You didn't mention it before.

SCOTT: It was just a stupid row. Have you ever been married?

GASKILL: My wife didn't end up murdered.

SCOTT: Oh, fuck you!

SCOTT goes to storm off. GASKILL stops him.

GASKILL: What did you argue about? The night she went missing.

SCOTT: I don't remember. Probably nothing.

RACHEL brings us back to the present.

RACHEL: You must remember.

SCOTT: ... If I told them now, they'd think I was hiding something.

RACHEL: If you haven't told them, then you *have* been hiding something.

SCOTT: Don't you people ever stop for a minute. Just one minute, to think about what this actually means for me? My wife's been murdered, and all the time everyone's looking at me, wondering if they're looking at a killer.

Oh God. Have you got a drink?

RACHEL: I'm not drinking now, I told you.

RACHEL rummages through the box.

RACHEL: Look, I have this. Someone bought it for me. I don't like it.

SCOTT: You don't like an eighteen-year-old single malt? You'd be a crap alcoholic.

RACHEL: What did you and Megan fight over?

SCOTT: *(Sipping from the bottle.)* That's good. Here, try some…

RACHEL: What did you argue about?

Lights take us into SCOTT and MEGAN's conversation.

MEGAN: **Come and sit with me. I need to talk to you.**

Beat.

MEGAN: **Scott, I…**

SCOTT: **Go on.**

MEGAN: **Look, I've made some mistakes.**

SCOTT: **What sort of mistakes?**

MEGAN: **Please don't make this any harder than it needs to be.**

SCOTT: ***(Grabs her arm.)* What sort of mistakes?**

MEGAN: **Don't raise your voice, Scott. It's not you.**

It was nothing. It's over now.

SCOTT: **But you've been seeing someone. Who?**

MEGAN: **It doesn't matter.**

SCOTT: **Who have you been fucking?**

MEGAN: **It doesn't matter. You don't know him.**

SCOTT: **Oh shit… I can't believe you could –**

MEGAN: **People have affairs all the time. It's the real world –**

SCOTT: **That's your excuse? People do it, so that makes it all right?**

MEGAN: **That's not what I'm saying –**

SCOTT: That you can apologise and everything's back to normal.

MEGAN: This isn't an apology. I'm not living the rest of my life trying to make it up to you. I messed up. I didn't understand what we had. But I'm drawing a line and moving on. Either we move on together, or –

SCOTT: How many? Since we've been together. How many men?

MEGAN: Don't do this.

SCOTT: So there've been more.

MEGAN: *(Lying.)* No.

SCOTT: Oh my God. How can I believe anything you say?

MEGAN: Please, it's over now. Listen, there's something important I have to tell you. But you have to forgive me before –

SCOTT: Forgive and that's it? 'Sorry about the affair.' 'Oh, never mind. Shall we have a cup of tea?'

MEGAN reaches for him, tenderly.

MEGAN: We can move forwards. I know we –

SCOTT: Don't touch me.

A stand-off neither know what to do. She reaches for him again and he fends her off. Suddenly, SCOTT grabs her by the hair. Drags her off.

MEGAN: You're hurting me.

He wrestles her across the room. Pushes her to the ground. His hand on her throat, holding her down. She fights back. Tears his t-shirt. Her fingernails down his torso. He grabs her hand.

SCOTT: I could crush you.

MEGAN: Please –

SCOTT: I could crush you like a fucking insect.

He doesn't hit her. She breaks free. She flees.

SCOTT brings us back to the present.

SCOTT: That was the last thing I said to her.

> How could I tell the police? They always think it's the husband at the best of times. I probably left bruises.

RACHEL: Was that the first time you'd hit Megan?

SCOTT: I didn't hit her. I just –

RACHEL: Left bruises.

SCOTT: Yes. It was the first time.

> Don't you think… Don't you think that after all the lying, all the…sleeping with someone else, aren't I allowed to react? Aren't I allowed to be hurt?

RACHEL: Yeah. You're allowed to be hurt.

SCOTT: That doesn't make me a murderer.

> *Beat.*

RACHEL: You always looked so happy together.

SCOTT: But she can't have been. Can she?

> *Beat.*

RACHEL: Is there anyone else the police suspect?

SCOTT: Gaskill did say he was looking into one suspect.

RACHEL: That's probably me.

SCOTT: So, here we are.

RACHEL: The two suspects.

> *Sharing the bottle.*

SCOTT: I can't face going back to the house. I keep catching myself, listening for her key in the door.

RACHEL: …

SCOTT: I forgot how hard I find being on my own. The house is so – [empty]

RACHEL: It's getting quite – [late]

SCOTT: There's no chance I could – [stay]

RACHEL: It's been a long – [day]

SCOTT: On the sofa, I mean. Just one night.

RACHEL doesn't want to commit.

SCOTT: Before she left, she was about to tell me something.
I keep thinking, what if…if she did really kill a child?
And there's no one we can ask now. Is there?

SCENE THREE

KAMAL ABDIC's home.

KAMAL: I don't usually have clients at my home.

RACHEL: Aside from Megan.

> *Beat.*

> *RACHEL enters.*

RACHEL: Have you seen what they've posted online?

KAMAL: I don't pay attention to it.

RACHEL: But you've seen it, right? That Megan had killed a child. People are saying she got what she deserved. What if that's the reason? The reason she was killed.

> *KAMAL doesn't want to hear it.*

RACHEL: Were you having an affair?

KAMAL: No! Look, yes, I'd developed feelings... I thought she felt the same. You saw the painting she gave me.

> She liked having someone who she could talk to about her art, about herself. Her husband, he didn't understand. I filled that space in her life. I confused it for something else.

> I went to hers, that Friday morning to tell her, to tell her that I found it too difficult to see her. I kissed her goodbye... And then I kissed her again. That's what you must have seen.

> Later, she turned up at mine. She said she wanted to finish her story. I thought I owed it to her.

RACHEL: What did she want to talk about? Craig McKenzie?

> *KAMAL hesitates.*

RACHEL: Did you tell the police about him?

KAMAL: She was found near her home. Not in Norfolk. It's not relevant –

RACHEL: Everything's relevant.

> *KAMAL hesitates.*

RACHEL: Why would you protect him?

KAMAL: I'm protecting Megan.

RACHEL: It's too late for that.

KAMAL: If you knew anything about her, you'd leave her in peace.

RACHEL: There are things about Megan that only you know.

KAMAL: It doesn't matter what I know.

RACHEL: If you do know something then you have to say. Otherwise, Megan's will be one of those names, one of those stories that dies away with no ending.

MEGAN appears.

MEGAN: I moved in with Craig when I was sixteen, into the cottage I told you about. It was at the end of a lane. Just Craig and me and the old railway track, the beach-grass and dunes. The restless sea.

KAMAL: You don't usually romanticise.

MEGAN: I know it doesn't sound like the sort of life I'd like but, after my brother died... All that mattered was that I was far from home. Where everything reminded me of Ben.

We used to have little fires on the beach. Craig would wrap me up in blankets and we'd watch the sea.

KAMAL: So what happened?

MEGAN: I got pregnant. It was too late, when I realised... We pretended it wasn't happening. Neither of us wanted it. I was only sixteen. I got bigger. Tired. We began to fight. I gave birth at home. We never even registered her. It was like she was a secret, right from the start.

I expected everything to be so hard, but it wasn't. I was surprised by how...maternal I felt. How complete. I used to lie there, with her on me, and we'd sleep. Sleep like I hadn't slept since Ben died.

I've wanted to tell someone this for so long.

KAMAL: Are you sure it's me you want to tell?

MEGAN: I have to finish my story.

KAMAL: I can refer you to someone else –

MEGAN: Please. I can't start again.

KAMAL: There's more to disclosure than just saying it.
Once it's out the bag, you can't put it back in. And
now – the way things are with us... You'll be dealing
with it on your own.

MEGAN: We deal with everything on our own. When it
comes to it. Let me tell you what happened, and then
I'll leave, and we can go back to our own lives.

I've kept this for so long, it feels like the words could
choke me in my sleep.

Please. Please, listen.

The baby. We called her Elizabeth. Libby.

One day, we had a fight, Craig and I. He walked out.
I remember the roof was leaking.

The sound of water, dripping into a bucket.

MEGAN: It was cold, the wind driving off the sea.
Whistling through the cracks in the window panes.
It'd been raining for days, we had no heating. I started
drinking, to warm up...but it didn't work so I filled the
saucepans and the kettle, to make a bath...

(Reliving it.) I got in, Libby with me, and it was so
warm. She lay on my chest, her head under my chin.

I can feel her.

There's a candle, flickering, just behind my head. I can
still smell the wax. Feel the chill of the air, round my
neck, my shoulders. I'm heavy. My body's sinking, into
the warmth, into the...and I'm so tired, I'm so...

When I wake up, I'm cold, really cold. The house feels
like it's shaking, the wind screaming, tearing at the
slates on the roof.

KAMAL: And Libby?

MEGAN: She was wedged between my arm and the edge of the tub. Her face in the water.

It was my fault. I killed her.

Scott wants us to have a baby. I keep putting him off but now...

How could I ever have a child? I lie there at night, still feeling her on me. I hear her crying. I smell her skin.

We buried her down by the disused railway line at the end of our garden. Beneath the daisies. I put my cardigan round her, I couldn't bear how cold she was. We used stones to mark her grave.

I never saw Craig again.

KAMAL: Did you ever try to find him?

MEGAN: Why would he want to see me? He must have nothing but hate for me.

KAMAL: Perhaps he left because he felt guilty too. He took in a young, vulnerable girl, and left her alone when she needed support.

If you did speak to him, you could forgive each other. Would that give you permission to forgive yourself?

MEGAN: I don't want to forgive myself.

KAMAL: Is it too late to try to find him?

MEGAN: You think I should?

KAMAL: It might help you understand that it wasn't all your fault.

He holds her.

MEGAN: Kamal, I'm / – [pregnant]

MEGAN's phone rings.

MEGAN: Hey. Yeah, I'm just with Tara... Yeah, I'm just heading off.

Okay.

I love you, too.

Megan hangs up.

MEGAN: **Sorry.**

Do you think I'm a monster?

KAMAL: **Monsters don't exist.**

MEGAN: **This is the last time I should see you. Isn't it?**

KAMAL: **It's the right thing to do. For you and Scott.**

MEGAN: **Will you be all right?**

KAMAL: **I'm a grown man.**

Beat.

MEGAN: **You're right. I'm going to find Craig. For closure.**

KAMAL: **Closure's a word you hear on daytime TV.**

You can't obliterate a memory. They're always there, in the shadows, sneaking into your dreams. In your case it would be about saying the things you never had a chance to say to him.

Back to the present.

KAMAL: She looked so hopeful, when she left. Like, she was finally able to...

RACHEL: Start living. You've got to tell the police all of this.

KAMAL doesn't want to.

RACHEL: It was you who led her to McKenzie. It makes sense, doesn't it? If he felt that she killed his baby.

(Seeing his distress.) Sorry. Look, I'm not blaming you. I'm not. She would have found him sooner or later.

If they found the body of the baby... Perhaps, Libby could be reburied with Megan. That'd be something, wouldn't it? You could make that happen. For Megan.

RACHEL goes to leave.

KAMAL: Rachel. You said, before, that you don't trust your memory.

RACHEL: Yes?

KAMAL: Do you trust yourself?

Beat.

KAMAL: The way to remember is to let yourself remember.

If that's really what you want.

RACHEL forces herself to go to the tunnel. Trying to remember.

SCENE FOUR

TOM's house. TOM stands next to a half-assembled baby's indoor swing.
He faces RACHEL.

RACHEL: It still feels like home.

TOM: Rach…

RACHEL: Like it's all been a big joke. As if Jeremy Beadle's about to jump out of a cupboard.

Is your wife in?

TOM: She's at the supermarket.

RACHEL: I just wanted to –

TOM: She'll be back soon. I've got to finish this *(meaning the swing)*.

RACHEL: Where was she Saturday night?

TOM: Here. I told you before, we had a night in. Had takeaway.

RACHEL: Tom. I saw her in the underpass. Your car. She couldn't have been in all night.

TOM: *(Really thinking.)* That can't be right.

RACHEL: How well do you really know her? Your wife.

TOM: Why are you doing this?

Silence.

RACHEL: *(Noticing something.)* You haven't changed that rug by the fireplace.

TOM: I still like it.

RACHEL: You do remember that we used to… [make love on it]?

TOM: Yes.

RACHEL: Do you still think about it?

TOM: No.

Beat.

RACHEL: How does it feel to you? That there's still pieces of me everywhere?

TOM: Look, I'm sorry –

RACHEL: Do you like it? Do you like thinking about me?

TOM: Rachel.

RACHEL: Do you think we tried hard enough?

TOM: We should have been more honest. Both of us.

I broke what we had – that was my fault. But we both were responsible for mending it.

RACHEL: D'you think we could have?

TOM: We'd stopped talking. Look, I promised Anna…

TOM goes back to the small swing. Struggling to get a piece to fit.

RACHEL: I always remember, on the way back from the hospital, after all the tests. You didn't hold my hand. I kept waiting for you to reach across, but you didn't.

Why didn't you?

TOM: I didn't know how to grieve. Or even if we were allowed to grieve for something that we never had.

RACHEL: I kept running over all the things I wanted to say. But we never spoke about it.

TOM: I just didn't know what to say.

RACHEL helps TOM with the baby's swing. RACHEL takes off her scarf, which has got in the way. At the end of the scene, it's left, lying on the ground.

RACHEL: I thought you blamed me.

TOM: No. *(Softly.)* I just – I hated being so powerless.

RACHEL: I can't believe this is the first time we're having this conversation.

TOM tightens the final bit. Job done. They stand. TOM presses a button on the swing. A lullaby plays and the swing begins, back and forth. Childless. They both watch. Silence. RACHEL wipes a tear. TOM stops the swing.

TOM: I'm really sorry, Rach.

RACHEL: I'm okay.

TOM: No, I mean… *(Awkward.)* Anna, she'll be back any minute.

RACHEL: I was trying really hard. I was helping with the Megan thing. I hadn't been drinking, and still my memory won't…

TOM comforts her.

RACHEL: And now I'm being evicted.

TOM: What? Why?

RACHEL: I lost my job. They sacked me.

TOM: When?

RACHEL: Six months ago. I turned up to a meeting drunk.

TOM: And you've just been pretending to go to work?

RACHEL: I'm going to have to live with my mum. Oh, God. My childhood bedroom.

TOM: You've just had a bad run. Look, if you need money, I'll transfer you some. It's just –

RACHEL: No –

TOM: It's just, you can't let Anna know.

RACHEL: It must be difficult for her. Living among the things we bought. Hanging her clothes on my coat hangers. Sleeping in the bed you and I chose. Lying there, knowing that used to be me, curled up with you. Holding you. Kissing you.

I really miss kissing you.

They look at each other. Finally, TOM backs away.

TOM: Please.

The sound of a car pulling up outside.

TOM: That'll be Anna. Just, try to look normal.

TOM goes to let her in. But it's GASKILL.

GASKILL: Well, look who's here!

RACHEL: …

GASKILL: Is Mrs Watson home? The second Mrs Watson.

TOM: Why?

A massive sigh from GASKILL. Exasperated!

GASKILL: Following up leads and…so on.

TOM: She's at the supermarket.

GASKILL: Oh! *(GASKILL makes a note in his pad.)* Supermarket.

TOM: What? What's wrong with that?

GASKILL: *(Showing him the pad.)* Oven chips. Don't want to forget.

Now, there was a sighting of your wife on the night Megan Hipwell went missing.

TOM looks at RACHEL.

GASKILL: Was your wife out and about on Saturday night?

TOM: No.

GASKILL: And what about you?

TOM: We were together. Watched a film.

GASKILL: What film?

TOM: *(Hesitates, then sheepish.) The Little Mermaid.*

It's the film Anna watches when she's upset.

GASKILL: So, you could vouch for Anna's whereabouts, could you?

TOM: Yeah, why?

GASKILL: Someone thinks they saw your car. A Peugeot.

TOM: There are thousands of Peugeots like ours.

GASKILL: Yours has one of those golf ball things on the aerial, doesn't it?

TOM: *(Confused.)* No.

GASKILL: It doesn't have one of those novelty aerial toppers?

RACHEL: I bought it for you, remember?

TOM: Yeah. But it fell off. Ages ago. You can check if you like.

A moment between RACHEL and GASKILL.

GASKILL: So, it wasn't your car in the underpass on Saturday?

TOM: No.

GASKILL: And you and Mrs Watson stayed in all night.

TOM: We've already told you all of this. After Rachel left, Anna and I had takeaway. I could probably find you the receipt if you're that concerned.

GASKILL: Nope. No need.

Look, it's my job to follow up all leads and possible sightings. No matter how far-fetched or *(looks at RACHEL)* crazy.

TOM: It's fine.

The sound of another car.

TOM: That's Anna. I'll go help her with the bags. And try to explain why you two are here. Again.

TOM leaves. GASKILL and RACHEL look at each other.

GASKILL: Tom invite you round for a quick drink, did he? Reminisce about the old days?

RACHEL: God, you're so annoying. I tell you something and you make out I'm the mad one. But here you are following up my lead.

GASKILL: How do you know I'm not just following you?

RACHEL: Because you know I'm right.

GASKILL: But you're not. Are you? Neither of them left the house – it wasn't even their car.

RACHEL: I'm sure it was her.

GASKILL: Like you were sure about Kamal Abdic; like you were sure about Craig McKenzie?

RACHEL: Have you found him?

GASKILL: Yep. Can't get a word out of him.

RACHEL: Why not?

GASKILL: Dead. Four years ago. Drugs.

RACHEL: So…

GASKILL: That brings us back to where we started.

RACHEL: What, Scott? There's no way Scott would have –

GASKILL: I'm not talking about Scott.

RACHEL: Oh, for goodness sake, if you think it's me, why not arrest me?

GASKILL: In cases like these, it's sometimes better to watch what people do. Let them dig up evidence for us. See if a grey beret turns up, for example. Or see if they return to the scene of the crime. Just passing Blenheim Road tonight, were you?

TOM comes in with all the shopping bags. ANNA carries nothing.

TOM: I was just explaining to Anna that, once again, our home has become the centre of attention.

RACHEL: Where's Evie?

ANNA: With my mum.

RACHEL: Oh…

ANNA: What does that mean, 'Oh…'?

RACHEL: Nothing. I'm not judging.

ANNA: Why would –

GASKILL: Mrs Watson.

ANNA/RACHEL: What?

Beat.

GASKILL: Anna. Before we come off track. Let me explain why I'm here, and then I'll leave you friends to it. Last Saturday. Just for the record: were you, at any point, out in your car?

TOM: You don't have to go through all this again.

ANNA: No. It's fine.

No. I was planning on going out with some friends, but, well, as you know, Rachel turned up here. Again. Uninvited. Again. After all of that, I just couldn't face it.

TOM: *(To GASKILL.)* All right?

GASKILL: Someone says they saw you in the underpass that night.

ANNA: *(Looking at RACHEL.)* I wonder who that could be.

RACHEL: I'm just saying what I saw.

ANNA: Through the bottom of a bottle.

RACHEL: You don't know anything about me.

ANNA: You don't know anything… Anything!

RACHEL: I know you were there.

ANNA: Why would anyone believe a thing you say?

RACHEL: Why would anyone believe a thing you…

Tom and I fucked on that rug.

Silence.

GASKILL: Well, I'll leave you to it. I'm sure you're all dying to catch up.

GASKILL leaves.

ANNA: You just can't leave us alone, can you?

RACHEL: I'm on my way to see Scott.

TOM: Rach, are you really sure you should see him?

ANNA: Why? Let him have her.

TOM: We still don't know who murdered Megan.

ANNA: What – Scott? Come on.

RACHEL: Why do you find it so hard to look after your own daughter?

ANNA: *(To TOM.)* Did you say that?

TOM: Of course not.

RACHEL: Some women would kill to have a baby. And you had to pay someone else to look after yours for you. You don't even have a job!

ANNA: You don't understand.

TOM: Anna got a bit tired. That's all. I thought, Megan might help.

ANNA: *(To TOM.)* I wasn't tired –

TOM: I just mean, having to get up all night. And all that fucking sterilising.

RACHEL: You didn't breastfeed?

ANNA: You have no idea what it's like! You can't even look after yourself!

Beat.

RACHEL: Why did Megan stop helping you? What happened?

ANNA: Nothing.

ANNA and TOM share a look.

RACHEL: Did she hurt Evie?

TOM: She was…she was just a bit cold.

ANNA: I should have known there was something wrong with her.

RACHEL: You don't know what she's been through. You don't have any right to –

ANNA: You didn't even know her. Or Scott.

RACHEL: He's invited me round for a drink, actually.

RACHEL turns to go.

TOM: You shouldn't go there alone –

RACHEL: Well, I'm going.

TOM: But, Rach –

RACHEL: No. I'm not your wife now – as you're all so keen to remind me. You don't get to tell me what to do anymore.

SCENE FIVE

SCOTT's house.

SCOTT: They've done the autopsy.

RACHEL: Did they find something?

SCOTT: Men. We're supposed to pretend we don't care about babies. Just football and beer for us.

She always found a reason to put it off. When she did agree, we did all the stuff you're meant to do. *(Wry.)* The ovulation sticks. The power foods. Vitamin supplements. A ban on drink!

RACHEL: Sometimes it just doesn't happen. It's no one's fault. Sometimes –

SCOTT: Gaskill asked me today. Asked if I knew that Megan was pregnant.

RACHEL: Oh, Scott.

Did they say how far along she was?

SCOTT: Twelve weeks. They've done a DNA test. *(Drinks purposefully.)* It's not mine.

Gaskill said the papers will have it by now.

RACHEL: Who cares what the papers say – what anyone says?

SCOTT: Because it'll be back on me! The jealous husband. Finds out his wife was pregnant, with her lover's child! You know how they put this stuff together.

RACHEL: No one who knew you would think that of you.

SCOTT: *You* don't know me!

RACHEL: I'm starting to.

SCOTT: You don't know anything.

They've found a little grave in a place called Holkham. Must be the child she killed.

RACHEL: But it was an accident! You should talk to Kamal Abdic –

SCOTT: Have you spoken to him?

RACHEL: No, I just – *(Lying.)* It was something Gaskill mentioned.

SCOTT: How d'you know Abdic wasn't lying? Maybe the papers are right about her.

RACHEL: Well, what was she like with Evie? She never hurt her, did she?

SCOTT: As far as I know.

RACHEL: Have you asked Anna?

SCOTT: Anna and Tom don't talk to me anymore. No one coming round with chicken and couscous now they think they might get bludgeoned to death for their trouble.

SCOTT drinks.

RACHEL: Why did Megan stop looking after Evie?

SCOTT: It had run its course. That's all.

RACHEL: There must have been a reason.

SCOTT: Anna got jealous of Megan floating around.

RACHEL: Anna was jealous of Megan?

SCOTT: You don't seriously think it was Anna? How could a woman have smashed Megan's head in, like that?

RACHEL: The same way a man could. With a brick, or something.

SCOTT: Anna had no reason to –

RACHEL: But if she felt threatened by Megan –

SCOTT: Rachel, whatever you might think of Anna, she isn't a murderer.

RACHEL: I'm sure I saw her, in the underpass, the night Megan disappeared.

SCOTT: What, you were there? Right near where Megan was found?

RACHEL: *(Realising SCOTT doesn't know this.)* I… I'd been to see Tom. It doesn't matter. The point is –

SCOTT: You never said that. You never said that you were there.

RACHEL: The point is, someone hit me.

SCOTT: Who?

RACHEL: I don't know.

SCOTT: What, attacking you? Or fending you off?

RACHEL: No! I don't remember.

SCOTT: You don't remember if you were attacking someone?

RACHEL: I don't remember what I remember –

SCOTT: How can you fucking not remember? What's wrong with you?

RACHEL: I can't…

SCOTT: You can't remember or you can't tell me?

RACHEL: I don't know. I don't know what to tell you.

Silence.

SCOTT: Does Gaskill know? That you were there.

RACHEL: I told him everything I saw, but, I passed out –

SCOTT: Jesus. And then you came here – what, two days later? With all your bullshit –

RACHEL: No, I told you –

SCOTT: Pretending you wanted to help me. You've been laughing at me, all along –

RACHEL: No –

SCOTT: That's what murderers do, isn't it? The psycho ones. They go back to their crimes. Befriend the relatives. Relive it over and over.

SCOTT grabs her. Pins her up against the wall.

RACHEL: Scott. Please –

SCOTT: You won't get away with it.

RACHEL: Why didn't you look for her, the night she went missing?

SCOTT: I could crush you like a fucking insect.

RACHEL freezes. We hear an echo of SCOTT saying that as before.

RACHEL: That's what you said to Megan.

Beat. RACHEL pulls away. Goes to leave.

SCOTT: Rachel –

RACHEL: No. I'm not taking it. Not from you or anyone. Not anymore.

SCOTT: … It's late. Let me to walk you to the station.

There might be someone dangerous out there.

RACHEL: I'll know to duck this time.

SCOTT: I didn't mean to… Let me walk with you.

RACHEL: *(Pushing him away.)* No. Megan's been found. I've told you and the police everything I know. That's it. I'm finished.

SCENE SIX

RACHEL back at her flat. Really loud thumping music. RACHEL drinking heavily. She's taking down her evidence/newspaper articles, increasingly aggressively. She finishes her drink.

She goes to one of her packed boxes. Rifles through it, chucking everything out. Eventually finds the bottle of whisky. Begins to slug from what's left.

The place is a complete mess. RACHEL too.

TOM appears.

TOM: What are you doing?

RACHEL: I've given up.

I have given up.

TOM: Rachel…?

RACHEL: No. All I've tried to do is help, and they all throw it back in my face, tell me I'm in the way. Tell me how shit I am. Even accuse me. And maybe they're right. I don't know what I did. I don't know what I'm capable of. As you constantly remind me. I'm scared… What if they are right?

TOM: Come on.

RACHEL: I thought I wasn't allowed to see you.

TOM: You left this at ours.

He hands her the scarf she left.

TOM: And, I wanted to tell you…You were right. It's not fair on Anna, having to live with so many shadows of us.

We're moving away.

RACHEL: You don't have to do that.

TOM: I can't keep getting close to you. Each time, I have to leave you all over again.

RACHEL: Where will you go?

TOM: …

RACHEL: Come on, Tom. It's me…

TOM: Looks like you're going too.

RACHEL: No choice.

TOM: I transferred you some money.

RACHEL: I pay this month's rent, what do I do next month?

TOM sighs. Begins to help RACHEL tidy up some of the mess, put stuff into her boxes.

TOM: Is that our…

RACHEL: What?

TOM: Our wedding album. *(Flicking through.)* You were really pretty. I mean, you still are, but, God, we looked so young… Not sure about your mum's hat.

TOM begins looking through stuff in the boxes. Picks out a top.

TOM: I always loved you in this.

RACHEL: When are you going?

TOM: We're putting the house on the market tomorrow, but, in the meantime, Anna wants us to rent somewhere. Just to – *(Stops dead.)*

RACHEL: What?

TOM pulls out of the box a grey beret. RACHEL stares at it.

RACHEL: I've never seen that before –

TOM: How did it get there?

RACHEL: I don't know –

TOM: But you know whose it is…?

RACHEL: I swear. I've never seen it before!

TOM: But you've seen the pictures on the news, the description of what she was wearing –

RACHEL can't believe it. Shock and horror.

RACHEL: Whatever you're thinking, don't think it.

TOM: Has anyone else been in your flat?

RACHEL: No. Just Gaskill. And Scott, but –

TOM: What have you done?

RACHEL: …

TOM: You said you had blood on your hands!

RACHEL: I had a cut! You've seen it.

TOM: How did you get it?

RACHEL: No, I told you –

TOM: Do you do it on purpose? Do you blank out these memories on purpose?

RACHEL: No!

TOM: Then you *have* to remember. This is all they'll need to convict you.

TOM puts the beret down.

RACHEL: You don't believe I did this. I know you don't.

TOM: Did you have any reason to hurt Megan?

RACHEL: I didn't even know Megan.

TOM: Come on. You need to remember.

RACHEL: I've tried. Bits come, but I can't trust them. Nothing fits.

TOM: You remember being at my house. Arguing with Anna…

RACHEL moves to the tunnel.

RACHEL: I was angry. With her, with you. He said it, the therapist, he said anger clouds memories.

TOM: Where did you go when you left mine?

RACHEL: I wanted more drink – for the train. I bought a bottle of wine… I called you, left a message, went through the underpass…

TOM: What about… What could you hear? Smells? Anything.

RACHEL moves towards the tunnel.

RACHEL: The chip shop. Salt and vinegar on the air. And it's cold. Sharp.

TOM: That's good. What else?

RACHEL: Music, from the pub.

TOM: Good. Was anyone there?

RACHEL: I can see someone. A woman.

TOM: D'you know her?

RACHEL: She looks familiar. Like, when you see someone from years ago, but can't quite place them.

MEGAN appears, wearing her grey beret.

RACHEL: Jess!

TOM: Who's Jess?

RACHEL: Megan. I thought it was Anna, but it was Megan I saw!

TOM: Stay in the moment. You see someone. Megan. Are you still angry?

RACHEL: Angry. I'd seen her, the day before. Cheating on her husband.

TOM: Do you say anything?

RACHEL: Wait!

MEGAN turns round.

RACHEL: Jess! Is that you?

MEGAN: Sorry?

RACHEL: I saw you, cheating on him!

MEGAN: I don't know you.

MEGAN walking away. The sound of a car door.

TOM: What else?

The sound of a train whooshing by.

RACHEL: I can't hear any words. She, yes, that was it, she was looking beyond me. Over my shoulder. Like, there was someone behind me. But –

TOM: There was no one there…

RACHEL: I didn't see anyone; I was looking at *her*.

TOM: And then what?

RACHEL: …

TOM: Come on. Everything you saw, it's in there somewhere. Did you call after her?

RACHEL: I think so. Yes. There was another train *(Sound of a train horn.)* I called again…but she…

TOM: Was she scared of you? A drunken stranger, shouting at her in the underpass.

RACHEL: I didn't want to hurt her. I just wanted to…

TOM: Concentrate, Rach. You're doing really well. What did you do?

RACHEL: I don't remember!

TOM: How can you not know what you've done?

RACHEL: Don't be cross with me.

TOM: Are you so ashamed of what you did, that you have to make yourself forget?

RACHEL: Just because I can't remember, it doesn't mean I did something bad…

TOM: It was always bad. I'd always have to tell you, the next morning, all the things you'd done. You never wanted to take responsibility.

RACHEL: How can I take responsibility for something I don't know I've done?

TOM: Because you still did it.

You kept saying you saw Anna in the underpass. Did you mistake Megan for Anna? You wanted to hurt her, the way she hurts you by being with me.

RACHEL: I don't know what I thought.

TOM: Was she scared?

RACHEL: Yes. Her eyes…

MEGAN: *(Horrified.)* What are you doing?

Sound of a bottle smashing.

RACHEL: I dropped my bottle of wine. *(Remembering.)* Someone hit me.

TOM: Megan.

RACHEL: I don't know. Yes. It must have been.

TOM: Because you'd been yelling at her. This blind filthy drunk girl, in her face. Then what?

RACHEL: I wouldn't have killed her.

TOM: Can you be sure that you didn't pour out all your bitterness and hatred onto that woman?

Silence. No. RACHEL can't be sure.

TOM: Can you picture yourself, with Megan, standing over her?

RACHEL: No. I don't know. Please, Tom –

TOM: Rachel. *(TOM physically composes RACHEL in position.)* Can you see yourself standing over her? Holding anything? A rock?

Were you hitting her? *(TOM now animates RACHEL, hit, hit.)*

They look at each other.

He pulls her into an embrace. RACHEL daren't move. It's chilling.

TOM: I'll look after you. The way I always did.

RACHEL doesn't know what to do.

Suddenly, someone at the door. TOM lets him in. GASKILL. He looks between TOM and RACHEL.

GASKILL: *(Knowingly.)* Is this a bad time?

(Seeing the half-packed bags.) Going somewhere in particular?

RACHEL: …

GASKILL: I always hoped it wouldn't go this way. But, well, I have to follow orders.

TOM: Look, Rachel's not feeling too good at the moment. Can you –

GASKILL: Well enough to pack her bags.

TOM's phone rings.

TOM: *(Answering the phone.)* Hey… Yeah, I've told her… Yeah, I'm off to the gym. *(Hangs up.)*

(To RACHEL.) I've really got to go.

(To GASKILL.) Don't push her. She's been through a lot.

Bye, Rach. Good luck.

A moment. TOM leaves.

GASKILL: And you can't tell me where you're going?

RACHEL: *(Discombobulated.)* What are you here for?

GASKILL: From the first time I saw you, the mess you were in, I felt for you. I did. Hoped you hadn't got yourself into trouble. But...

I've got this warrant to search your house. *(He begins to look through her stuff.)* No need to bring the cavalry. I'm sure you won't obstruct –

She fumbles with some keys. She bolts. We hear her lock her door, from the outside, before GASKILL can catch her.

GASKILL: Rachel! Unlock the door!

GASKILL pounds on the door. Darkness. The sound of rain.

SCENE SEVEN

ANNA and TOM's house. ANNA has a glass of wine. RACHEL bursts in.

RACHEL: Where's Tom?

ANNA: What are you –

RACHEL: Where's Tom?!

ANNA: He was going to the gym, after yours. He forgot his bag, so he'll be –

RACHEL: Where's Evie?

ANNA: That's none of your –

RACHEL: Come on –

ANNA: Asleep. Upstairs.

RACHEL: Look, you don't like me. I get that. I'm not your biggest fan either, but you've got to leave.

ANNA: What?

RACHEL: You've got to get Evie and leave. Right now. Before he comes back.

ANNA: What are you talking about?

RACHEL: It's Tom! Tom killed Megan.

ANNA: You've been drinking.

RACHEL: Megan's hat went missing when she was killed. It just turned up in my flat. In one of my boxes.

ANNA: Then, it was you…

RACHEL: Tom had just been going through them, looking at my stuff.

ANNA: So?

RACHEL: So, he planted it there. He must have done.

ANNA: Rachel, ever since Megan was found, you've been saying it was *me*. You told everyone you saw me in the underpass. My car.

RACHEL: Your car. The golf ball. Where's that golf ball thing on your aerial?

82

ANNA: Tom took it off.

RACHEL: When?

ANNA: When you and Gaskill were here. He came to help me in with the shopping. He just took it off.

RACHEL: You didn't ask why?

ANNA: I didn't think anything of it. I always hated it.

RACHEL: I'd just identified it to Gaskill – in front of Tom. Ask him. Ask him why it was so important to remove it from your car.

ANNA: *(Gestures to the gym bag.)* He'll be back any minute; ask him yourself.

RACHEL: And you're in no doubt he's going to the gym?

They look at the bag. RACHEL goes to it, opens it. A gym kit. Water bottle. A mobile phone.

RACHEL: *(Holding the phone.)* Whose is this?

ANNA: Tom's. He must have left it.

RACHEL: But you called him on his phone when he was at mine.

RACHEL turns on the phone.

RACHEL: Don't you want to know?

A moment, and then the phone beeps. RACHEL presses a button. Looks at the texts.

RACHEL: Texts. *(Reads.)* MONDAY, 3 P.M. MINE? KISS. Sender says: NO. ANNA WILL BE BACK BY THEN. So, it's Tom!

Other person says, OKAY. MAKE IT 2.

ANNA: Who's the other person?

RACHEL: No name. And look, this one, sent last Friday: the sender says: 4.30, TODAY QUESTION MARK. Tom replies: CAN'T. WHAT ABOUT SATURDAY MORNING. AT THE GYM?

Did Tom go to the gym Saturday morning?

ANNA: …

RACHEL: Did he?

ANNA: … How do we find the name?

RACHEL: I don't – Wait…

RACHEL fumbles for her own phone. Checks the number against one in her phone.

RACHEL: Scott typed Megan's number into my phone when we were looking for her. Look…

ANNA doesn't want to look.

RACHEL: You have to look.

Reluctantly, ANNA looks.

RACHEL: Text after text. To Megan.

ANNA turns away. Doesn't want to look.

RACHEL: Did you know he was having an affair with her?

ANNA: …

RACHEL: He'd tell you he was going out, wouldn't he? With his army friends. Did *you* ever meet them?

Or he'd have all these phone calls, late at night. Tell you stuff was kicking off at work.

Silence.

RACHEL: You have to get out of here –

ANNA: None of that means he killed her.

RACHEL: Why would he plant the hat at my house?

ANNA: How do I know you haven't concocted this whole thing? The things you're capable of. You took my baby.

RACHEL: I didn't take your baby. I came round, the door was open, you were asleep and Evie was crying. I picked her up, to soothe her –

ANNA: Tom said you were standing on the railway tracks with her –

RACHEL: I was in the garden.

ANNA: But Tom said –

RACHEL: Tom lies. Anna. Tom always lies. And he gets you to lie.
I just wanted to feel the weight of his baby, in my arms.

A moment of understanding.

RACHEL: His car in the underpass. The aerial topper. The affair
with Megan. The secret phone. The way he was with me.
And now the way he is with you.

ANNA: You've no idea what he's like with me.

RACHEL: Watching you is like watching an actor playing my
life. Who poured you that glass of wine?

ANNA: …

RACHEL: That's how it started with me. I never used to drink at
home. Tom would pour a glass for me and leave the bottle.
He'd be gone for hours, so I'd have another. He called me
an alcoholic.

Tell me he isn't doing that with you.

ANNA: …

RACHEL: He tells you, you can't cope and soon you begin to
feel it…don't you?

ANNA can't say – but we see her acknowledge that RACHEL's right.

RACHEL: I'll call the police.

RACHEL gets out her mobile and dials 999. ANNA stops her.

RACHEL: Even without all this [evidence], you know, don't you?

The sound of a car pulling up outside. TOM. They both hear it.

ANNA: It wasn't him. It can't have been. *(Decisively.)* He was
here. All night.

RACHEL: That can't be true.

ANNA: He didn't leave the house, not even for a second. So
you're wrong.

RACHEL: Why are you trying to protect him? He's –

TOM comes in. Looks between them.

ANNA: *(Reeling, trying to act normal.)* Where have you been?

TOM: To the gym. I forgot my bag. So I –

RACHEL: You left my place before me; how come you've only just got here?

TOM: I…drove all the way there before I realised. *(To Anna.)* What's all this about?

Anna?

ANNA: She thinks it was you.

TOM: What?

ANNA: That it was you who killed Megan. But I told her you were here, all night. That you never left the house.

RACHEL: *(To TOM.)* I see what you've been doing. What you always did. Make me feel ashamed and guilty, and then tell me what I'd done, until I believed you.

TOM: What are you talking about?

RACHEL: The therapist, he said how we can construct memories. That's what you used to do to me! Always telling me I'd had too much to drink while pouring me more. Telling me I was blind filthy drunk.

TOM: You *were* always –

RACHEL: Like that time with the golf club. The next morning you put the club in my hands and showed me how I'd tried hitting you. But it was you, wasn't it? You who'd swung for me. You forced the memory on me until it became real.

TOM: *(To ANNA.)* She's making it up –

RACHEL: You've been having an affair with Megan.

TOM: That's ridiculous.

RACHEL shows him the phone.

RACHEL: Anna's seen the texts.

TOM: Anna, honestly, I can explain it –

RACHEL presses the voicemail.

VOICEMAIL: You have one saved message. Message received Saturday, six fifty-nine p.m.

MEGAN: *(On the voicemail.) (Crying, desperate.)* Tom, it's me. Scott and I have just had a massive argument. You have to meet me right away. Meet me in the underpass. There's something I've got to tell you.

RACHEL presses a button.

VOICEMAIL: Message saved.

TOM grabs the phone.

TOM: She asked, but that doesn't mean I went to meet her.

RACHEL: *(To ANNA.)* Get Evie. We have to get out of here.

RACHEL goes to leave. TOM blocks her way.

TOM: You're not going anywhere until you've told the truth.

RACHEL: We know it was you. We both know.

TOM: Anna. I promise you. I did not kill her.

ANNA: …

RACHEL: You just planted Megan's hat at mine!

TOM: *(Thinking on his feet.)* I asked you who else had been to your flat. You said that Gaskill had been there, and who else?

RACHEL: … Scott.

TOM: Did he touch your boxes, your bags?

RACHEL: Yes, but –

TOM: I warned you. I can't believe I let you go to see him on your own –

RACHEL: But…it was you. I know it was.

TOM: Has Scott ever been threatening towards Megan?

RACHEL knows that SCOTT <u>has</u> been threatening.

TOM: That's why he and Megan had that massive argument! And he left that vile message on her phone that night.

RACHEL: *(Clocks something… Spins the web.)* … Yeah. Gaskill told me. Scott said something…

TOM: Called her a lying bitch. He said he could kill her.

Beat.

RACHEL: How did you know Scott left that message on her phone?

ANNA: Tom…?

RACHEL: There's no way you could have known what message he left on her phone unless you were with her that night. You had to have been.

(To ANNA.) Get Evie and let's go.

TOM stops RACHEL from leaving.

TOM: You're not doing this. You're not ruining my life again.

RACHEL: *(To ANNA.)* Ask him. Ask him why he killed Megan.

TOM: *(To ANNA.)* I didn't kill her. Yes, I'm sorry. I should never have let Megan get her claws into me. It didn't mean anything. I told her I didn't want anything more to do with her. That I loved my family.

RACHEL: But she called you on Saturday night and you went running to her.

(To ANNA.) And he's using you as his alibi.

ANNA: What did she tell you?

TOM: What?

ANNA: Megan. On the message, she said she had to tell you something?

TOM: She wanted me to be with her. I said no. Then she said, she said she'd murdered a child. She threatened to harm Evie. I told her, I wouldn't be blackmailed.

RACHEL: Megan didn't murder a child, it was an accident.

TOM: *(To ANNA.)* Why would you believe her?

RACHEL: That's why she was in therapy –

TOM: Don't listen to her. She doesn't even know Megan –

RACHEL: I know Megan was pregnant. That's what she told you. That she was pregnant.

TOM: …

RACHEL: She told you, right? *(RACHEL realising.)* It wasn't
Scott's, and she'd never slept with Kamal. It was yours.

TOM: *(To ANNA.)* This is just her – you know what she's like,
making shit up and throwing it at innocent –

RACHEL: There would have been no hiding that it wasn't Scott's.

TOM turns to ANNA.

TOM: Anna, all I want is for you and Evie and me to live how
we said. Move away. Just the three of us. Like you always
wanted.

TOM tries to take ANNA's hand but she doesn't let him.

EVIE cries, offstage.

TOM: Okay, I did go to meet her. Just quickly, when I went to
get our takeaway. I pulled up in the car. And who should
be staggering towards us. *(To RACHEL.)* The fucking state of
you… Shouting at her –

MEGAN: *(To TOM.)* What are you doing?

The sound of smashing glass.

RACHEL: *(Realising.)* It was you who hit me.

TOM: You were threatening Megan. All I did was push you off
her –

RACHEL: You hit me over the head. *(Points to the cut on her head.)*
(To ANNA.) Look what he's really like!

EVIE cries again.

TOM: I'll make this right. I swear. It'll be just us. Where she
can't find us. What you always wanted.

RACHEL: How could you bring Evie up with him?

TOM: Don't listen to her. I'm a good father. You know I am.

RACHEL: What kind of life would you have?

TOM: Evie loves me. She needs me. Go upstairs to her.

EVIE cries louder.

TOM: *(To ANNA.)* I swear to you, I didn't kill Megan.

RACHEL: Anna, please –

TOM: Go to her, darling. Go to our daughter.

    Beat.

    ANNA goes.

RACHEL: There's no point lying to me.

TOM: … I told her to get rid of it.

    I begged and begged but she wouldn't listen—

**MEGAN: *(Separate from RACHEL and TOM, haunting.)* I just
had the twelve-week scan. She was sucking her thumb.**

TOM: I was just trying to make her understand *(He uses RACHEL
as an actor in his re-enactment. Holding her by the arms.)*

MEGAN: That's when I decided…

TOM: I told her:

MEGAN: I'm not going to be anyone's secret anymore.

TOM: 'I won't let you destroy my family.'

MEGAN: My baby will not be someone's unwanted baggage.

RACHEL: *(Simultaneously.)* Let me go –

MEGAN: *(Simultaneously.)* Let me go –

TOM: I can't let you go until you see sense.

MEGAN: I'm not killing my baby!

    RACHEL breaks free of TOM.

    In MEGAN's world, she too, breaks free, fit to run.

TOM: Get back! /

TOM: *(Audio.)* Get back!

    TOM grabs RACHEL.

    ***In MEGAN's world, mirroring RACHEL, she too is grabbed.
Her beret falls aside. The sound of magpies.***

TOM: *(Getting over RACHEL.)* If you weren't like one of those
unwanted dogs that keeps coming back no matter how
much you punish them…

If you hadn't come round that night, none of this would have happened… All of this, is your fault.

RACHEL: No. You killed her.

RACHEL reaches for the corkscrew.

RACHEL: No one but you.

RACHEL stabs TOM's arm. He lets go. She runs outside.

Rain. Dark. Mist. TOM chases, grabs RACHEL by the hair.

TOM: Do you have any idea how boring you became?

They are now down near the railway line. Mist near the tunnel. The sound of a train, in the distance.

TOM: Too sad to get out of bed, too tired to wash your hair?

The sound of the train growing nearer.

ANNA has appeared.

RACHEL: That's not who I was. That's not who I am.

TOM has his hands round RACHEL's throat, strangling her.

ANNA runs up. ANNA tries to pull TOM off RACHEL.

Train's headlights appear in the tunnel. Very loud.

In the tussle, RACHEL and ANNA face TOM. They both push him into the oncoming train. Bang.

Train's horn. The train's headlights whizz past, into the audience. And they're gone.

When the mist settles, all that remains: TOM's ripped clothes, lying on the ground.

RACHEL and ANNA hold each other. The gentle murmuring of EVIE crying.

GASKILL turns up. Shocked silence.

SCENE EIGHT

RACHEL's flat. Tidy.

GASKILL: Just think, if you'd have had a decent book to read on the train, none of this would have happened. Funny really.

RACHEL: Funny's not quite the word I'd use.

GASKILL: No…

RACHEL: Although, I suppose it's not every day you end up killing someone, trying to prove you're not a killer.

But…you saw it, right? You saw that it was self-defence?

GASKILL doesn't commit.

GASKILL: Anna's given her statement, which tallied with yours. Tom was attacking you both and you pushed him away. She said you were there trying to help her and her baby. That'll stay on record.

You'll have to give your statement in court. Say all of this under oath.

RACHEL: But there's no doubt Tom killed Megan.

GASKILL: His DNA was on the hat. The messages on his secret phone. And Megan's unborn baby, that was Tom's. It all paints a pretty clear picture.

RACHEL: And you'll give your statement?

GASKILL: … *(Makes his decision.)* Lucky for you I was there.

RACHEL: A reliable witness.

GASKILL: At last!

They smile.

RACHEL: How's Scott?

GASKILL: … Megan was buried yesterday. In Holkham, with the remains of the child they found. Some consolation, I suppose.

RACHEL: You were there?

GASKILL: *(Nods.)* Just Scott and a few others. A day by the sea.

Pause.

RACHEL: Did you really think it was me?

GASKILL: I just follow the evidence.

How are you doing now?

RACHEL: Yeah. All right, actually.

GASKILL: We can arrange for you to see someone. If you need to talk about it.

RACHEL: I'm tired of living in the past.

What will you do now?

GASKILL: A few days off. Going to Yorkshire. National Railway Museum.

RACHEL: With anyone?

GASKILL: Well... I like my own company.

RACHEL: Sounds nice.

GASKILL: Yeah. Change of scenery. Maybe you should go, sometime.

RACHEL: Yeah. Maybe I will.

Pause.

GASKILL: You still moving away?

RACHEL: Not right now. I've got a job interview. It's a bit of a commute.

GASKILL: Ah! Stare into the back of someone else's house.

RACHEL: *(Smiles.)* But I like the train. The feeling of getting somewhere.

GASKILL: The soothing rhythm.

RACHEL: Strangers smiling at text messages.

GASKILL: Couples asleep on each other's shoulder.

RACHEL: Sharing a moment with the person opposite when your feet accidentally touch. The pleasure of helping a mother with a pushchair. The darkness of a tunnel, turning the windows to mirrors – and the light at the end of it. The blur of debris between the tracks and the back gardens. The speed of the world standing still. And the back windows – other lives being lived. Bedsheets hung as curtains; forgotten flowers, dying in a vase.

And maybe, in one of those houses, someone looking out at the passing train…wondering, wondering who those passengers are, who'll be waiting for them when they get home. Dinners being cooked. Dogs waiting to hear the key in the door. Children waiting for a story and a goodnight kiss. A man on the train, loosening his tie. A child on the train, drawing a pattern on the steamed-up window. And a girl on the train…a *woman* on the train, choosing not to get off at her station. Staying on, scared, but moving forward. Alone, but complete. Stronger than she ever knew. Moving on. Moving on. Not looking back.

WWW.OBERONBOOKS.COM